Praise for
ADOPT WITHOUT DEBT

"I receive calls on my show all the time about how you have to go into debt to adopt. Julie Gumm is living proof and a testament to the fact you can adopt without ANY debt. I highly recommend reading *Adopt Without Debt* if you are considering adoption."

- Dave Ramsey, Best-selling author, national speaker and nationally-syndicated talk radio host

"I've been waiting for a book like this for almost a decade now. The reality has been that finances are often the biggest obstacle to adopting a child. Thanks to Julie Gumm that reality is going to change. *Adopt Without Debt* should be read by every prospective adoptive couple. It's that helpful."

- Dan Cruver, Director of Together for Adoption

"At Project HOPEFUL we often receive letters from families who desire to adopt but are concerned about funding. I highly recommend *Adopt Without Debt* as a must-read for any adoptive parent looking to discover creative ways to afford their adoption. The ideas in this book work!"

- Carolyn Twietmeyer, Founder & Executive Director of Project HOPEFUL

D0066900

Adopting a child without going into debt really is possible. We have families that do it every day (and you can, too!). Julie's book *Adopt Without Debt* is packed with resources, fresh income raising ideas and cost-saving spending habits – all of which are delivered by an author with successful first-hand experience and a heart for the widow and the orphan. Highly recommended!

- Jennifer Newcomb, Communications Coordinator with Children's Hope International

The story she tells in this book of getting debt-free and affording adoption in the process is inspirational. If you're wondering how your family might be able to afford to adopt, this book might very well provide some new insight.

- Mary Ostyn, Author *Family Feasts for $75 a Week*, adoptive mom

Julie makes the cost of adoption manageable and, prayerfully, "Adopt Without Debt" will allow many more families to embark on this incredible journey. Great resource for any family in the adoption process.

- Emily Alexander, Founder - Hope for Dube Bute, adoptive mom

ADOPT WITHOUT DEBT

Creative Ways to Cover
the Cost of Adoption

JULIE GUMM

REVISED & EXPANDED

Adopt Without Debt: Creative Ways to Cover the Cost of Adoption
Published by Black Boot Publishing
P.O. Box 6341
Goodyear, AZ 85338

Second Edition, First Printing

Cover Design by Cameron Smith
Cover Photography by Kimmybee Photography
Scripture © New International Version

ISBN: 978-0-9835398-2-7

Orders: www.adoptwithoutdebt.com

Connect with the Author
Email: julie@adoptwithoutdebt.com
Twitter: @jgumm
Facebook: facebook.com/adoptwithoutdebt

Printed in the United States of America

For Wendemagegn & Beza
Who opened their hearts and let me be their Mom.

For Noah & Natalie
Who embraced their new brother and sister.

For Mark
Who listened to God - and your crazy wife.

Acknowledgements

Thank you to all the adoptive families who shared their stories with me. It was inspiring to talk with others who have the same heart for orphans.

I am grateful for all the support and excitement shown by countless friends, particularly my amazing cheerleading squad - Jen, Stacey and Kristen. Your anticipation and joy helped fuel me. Your gentle (and not so gentle) nudges kept me going even when doubts interrupted me. I love that you are as excited about my first book as I am.

My brother, Phil, and my dad, Nat, spent MANY hours editing and made my words even better. Thank you for toiling over my project as if it were your own.

One of the first copies of this book goes to Gary Warner, my John Brown University journalism professor. I'm a little scared he'll get out his red pen, but since he is retired, maybe I'm safe. More than just the mechanics of writing and editing, Mr. Warner taught me to never settle for hurried and uninspired writing - but to do this thing that I love, writing, with excellence. I am forever grateful.

Mom and Dad, thank you for always believing I was capable of great things. I've come a long way from the little girl who used to write notes and stuff them in Dad's sock drawer. I could not have done it without your love and support.

To the rest of my immediate family - Brad, Suzanne, Phil, Tricia, Billy, Cathy, Matt, Hollie, Jenny and Rob - God gave me the greatest gift when he put each one of you in my life. Each of you fills a special role and has played a vital part in our adoption journey. Thank you for your love and support.

Luke, Noah, Beza and Natalie - thanks for putting up with me during this crazy process. We will now return to our normally-scheduled life.

To Mark, my husband of 18 years, I love you! The 20-year-old girl who stood beside you in front of that church had NO idea of the wild ride on which God would take us, but I wouldn't trade it for anything. You are my rock, my partner in parenting and ministry, and I couldn't do life without you. Thank you for all the mornings you let me sleep in until 11 after a late night of writing, for all the loads of laundry and for all the nights you put up with leftovers because I had no energy left. I look forward to what God has for us with amazement, excitement and anticipation.

At the heart of this book is a simple message that God continues to whisper in our ears, "Follow me, I will provide." Mark and I have experienced that truth countless times in our marriage, but never as profoundly as during our adoption process. I am amazed and humbled that He would use me to share that message with others. A line in one of my favorite songs echoes in my heart "Forever, You are the God of my story. Write every line for Your glory." That is my simple prayer.

Table of Contents

Introduction

There is a global orphan epidemic, which left unchecked will change the course of future generations–and not for the better!

Many children live today without the nurturing love of parents and a family.

Yet, we seem to be on the cusp of a revolution - of couples, families and single adults that stand up to say, "Yes, I will make a difference. I will be a family for these children."

Adoption alone will not solve the global orphan crisis, but it is a key component to fulfilling a large, complicated need.

Each year thousands of children are placed in families through private adoption attorneys, licensed adoption agencies and state foster-care systems.

But thousands more might find homes if people understood one thing.

You CAN afford it!

Despite scary looking amounts of $15,000-$40,000,

adoption doesn't require a second mortgage or maxed-out credit cards.

Over 115,000 kids in the United States hunger for a mom, a dad, and a real family. Through the state, you can adopt these kids into your family for little or no cost. Only a few hundred dollars stands between them and the hope of a loving future.

For those pursuing private or international adoption, hope exists for you as well. Over a dozen grant organizations exist to help adoptive families, and there are countless other ways you can raise the money to bring a child into your family. This book will show you how.

Studies have shown that hundreds of thousands of families have considered adoption but have NEVER followed through. Why? Most likely, out of fear, with the cost of adoption toward the top of the list.

My prayer is that this book will help you overcome that one fear.

The cost of adoption should never stand in the way of giving a child a family.

COMMITMENT, CHANGE & CHILDREN

Our Adoption Story

1
Dave, Debt & Destiny

People often ask, "When did you first decide to adopt?" Truth is I can't pinpoint an exact time. The idea of adoption kind of crept into our lives.

In high school, I worked for two years for an adoption attorney who handled both private adoptions and court-appointed legal matters for children in the state foster system. Typing his legal briefs and court papers opened my eyes to both the incredible heartache in some of the children's lives, as well as the joy of the chosen adoptive parents.

Eight years later Mark and I were married and ready to start our own family. After a year and no pregnancy, I wondered if perhaps God intended that early experience to prepare me for an adoption journey of our own.

Turns out all I needed was a little more patience - six months later I was pregnant with our son, Noah, who arrived in 1999. In 2002, our daughter Natalie joined the family. At the time of her birth, we hadn't really decided how many kids we wanted. When we first married, we

wanted two, but during the second pregnancy, we began
to think that maybe three was the right number. Later
that year, overwhelmed with two kids (and what doctors
would later diagnose as clinical depression) I declared
myself D-O-N-E! I had a boy and a girl, and I was good.
Our family was complete.

During this same time, however, our family had
embarked on another journey. While seemingly unrelated
to adoption, it was really a major catalyst.

In 2000, Mark and I attended a Dave Ramsey Financial
Peace Live seminar (now called "Dave Ramsey Live").
Inspired, Mark and I set out to gain control of our finances
and become debt free. We were still young - 28 and 27
respectively - and excited about what a debt-free future
would mean.

While I didn't dream of palatial mansions and exotic
cars, I will admit the allure of being debt free involved
retiring at age 50, traveling the world and renting a house
on the beach every summer. Of course, more practical
matters - like being able to pay cash for our kid's college -
didn't really excite me the way it did Mark.

We attacked our debt - credit cards, and car and
student loans - with the "gazelle intensity" Ramsey
describes.

We adjusted our lifestyle and re-prioritized our
spending habits. It's not that we lived on beans and rice,
but eating out became a treat, not a weekly occurrence. We
downgraded the satellite package, and I cut back on my
shopping sprees. We put off large purchases like the big
screen TV, saving for them over time and discovering that

when we had the cash, sometimes the purchase no longer seemed important.

Within 12 months, we paid off the student loans, paid off the credit cards, paid off one car, and sold the other car that still had a large loan. While we planned to purchase an inexpensive used car, we were given my grandmother's car when she died. It was a 1991 Buick Century. Not exactly our dream car but it had been well maintained and had low mileage. We were ready to swallow our pride if it meant freedom.

It wasn't always easy, but as we whittled away at our debt, the freedom and excitement just motivated us even more.

Having those debts paid off was the most amazing feeling! Next, we built up our savings so we would never have to borrow money again.

With our house refinanced on a 15-year mortgage, we envisioned ourselves debt free at ages 43 and 42.

We'd faithfully given to our church for several years. But now that we didn't have $1,300 a month in consumer debt, we could support friends who were missionaries, sponsor children across the world and adopt local needy families for Christmas.

We began to shift our financial outlook a second time.

Suddenly using our money to help others became way more fun than spending it on ourselves.

I'm not going to lie; I like a shopping trip as much as the next girl. But as we loosened our hold on our money, we could see God's direct blessings over and over again.

In 2002, working full time and pregnant with our

daughter, I realized how little time I spent with Noah who was in full-time daycare. It weighed heavily on my heart; for the first time, I was ready to walk away from my career.

With Mark working as a Christian school teacher, losing two-thirds of our household income wasn't going to be easy. But we resolved to do it. We had already learned to live on less and had no consumer debt payments, but it was still going to be a big challenge.

Yet God showed his goodness and blessing. I kept my job in a part-time, work-from-home capacity and Mark accepted a new job with our church.

While it would have been nice to sock money away in a 401(k) or pay down our home mortgage, we were happy I could stay home. Still, we kept our 2015 debt-free goal in mind.

Then in 2003, the housing market went nuts. It went a little crazy everywhere, but it went REALLY crazy in Phoenix. Houses went on the market for double their purchase price and buyers snapped them up in days, sometimes hours.

Mark started crunching numbers and researching - something he loves. Me? I was cringing at the thought of moving again. (Three moves in five years wears on a girl, you know!)

At the time, most people sold their homes for a ridiculous price and then bought an equally over-priced home in a better neighborhood. I wondered what the point was. I loved our house and our neighborhood.

But Mark discovered that prices on houses farther out of town had not risen as much - especially on new construction. By downsizing and moving 13 miles west, we could grab an incredible opportunity.

The math showed us that we could sell our current house, put the profit (saving out money for moving, landscaping, etc) down on a new house and shrink our mortgage dramatically. We looked at our budget and saw that if we really buckled down and attacked that mortgage, we could pay it off in two to three years.

Suddenly, debt-free at 43/42 became debt-free at 35/34. So we went for it!

Turns out, it was the best financial decision we EVER made.

- - - - - - - - - -

During this time, my husband worked on staff with our church, among other things, overseeing the benevolence funds and developing an interest in missions and helping people in need.

I continued, as I had for years, to find myself moved by news stories of kids in foster care, kids rescued from abusive situations and stories of adoption.

I think I even mentioned to Mark that MAYBE we should consider doing short-term emergency foster care. But I was still scared of something more permanent. I envisioned having children for a few days until social services found them permanent foster homes. I was too scared to think beyond that.

But life continued and nothing changed.

At the same time, God started working in Mark and

really developing his gift of mercy and compassion. He traveled to Mississippi with a church team in the wake of Hurricane Katrina - a trip that would greatly change his life.

In 2006, Mark met a pastor from Zambia and started looking into a possible missions project - an orphanage - for our church. When our pastor asked in passing, "Can you adopt from Zambia?" I started some research online. From there, I was pretty much a goner - adoption had taken root in my heart.

One day Mark was reading his Bible in James and he stopped when he read James 1:27.

> *"Religion that God our Father accepts as pure and faultless is this: to look after orphans and widows in their distress and to keep oneself from being polluted by the world."*

"Do I even know one single orphan?" Mark thought to himself. When he realized he didn't, his heart broke. If caring for widows and orphans in their distress is so close to God's heart, how could we have been so ignorant of His command.

Mark processed all these thoughts internally. We hadn't yet talked with each other about orphans or adoption.

Meanwhile, God continued to gently place the fatherless in front of us - news stories, movies and blogs. It's really pretty funny when I think about it now. It took me a LONG time to really get the message.

Then in May 2007, good friends of ours, Dustin & Jen Sloniger, announced they had decided to adopt. My ears perked up. I think I even said, "I've thought about doing that."

Over the next four months, I researched international adoption, peppered Jen with questions and percolated on the idea. Yet Mark and I still hadn't really discussed it together. I think I was still figuring out if I really wanted to bring this up - I was still afraid of going down the adoption path.

Yet I couldn't really leave it alone.

2
Ships, Songs & Savings

In early October 2007, Mark attended the Catalyst conference with several church staff members. Dave Ramsey was one of the keynote speakers and during his session he shared a video interview with a couple that wanted to adopt. Determined to pay off their debt first, the family had a chance encounter with another couple who offered to pay off their debt so they could start the adoption process. I wasn't there, but I'm pretty sure the video made Mark cry. He left telling a friend, "I want to be that guy."

When he sent me a link to the video, I wasn't sure if that meant he wanted to be the guy adopting or the guy paying off the debt. Either way, I saw that God was working on him as well.

A few weeks later, Mark and I were eating lunch at Chipotle, sitting outside enjoying the beautiful Phoenix fall weather. Halfway through the meal, I blurted out, "So what do you think about adopting?"

I expected Mark to fall off the chair or, at the very least, laugh at me. When he didn't, we started talking about what God had whispered to both of us separately.

A few weeks later, we cruised the Mexican Riviera - just the two of us. It was a celebratory occasion - we had made the FINAL house payment that month. We were debt free!

In my suitcase, I had packed brochures from a dozen different adoption agencies and printed pages of online adoption research.

By the time we came home, we had decided "yes," we were going to adopt. With Natalie starting kindergarten the next fall, we didn't think we wanted to adopt young kids. We felt like we were done with that part of our lives. Plus we knew that older children are often harder to place. We knew sibling sets were even harder to place.

We still didn't know from where we would adopt. We were both drawn to international adoption. I was leaning toward Africa. Mark thought maybe China.

In the end, God led us right to our children.

- - - - - - - - - -

During my requests for information from agencies, I connected with a non-profit organization working in Ethiopia. I asked for access to their waiting child list; they informed me that they had just returned from a trip to Ethiopia and would have a new DVD of waiting children soon. I asked them to send it.

The DVD came, and late one night in December I popped it into my computer and briefly scanned the disc menu. By that point, we had decided we wanted a sibling group between the ages of five and eight (our kid's ages at the time). We intended to keep Noah as the oldest child, which we thought would be important to him. We were open to two boys, or a boy and a girl. (Noah vetoed TWO girls!)

I watched a few miscellaneous clips, but there were two sibling sets that fell within that five to eight range.

I clicked on the first one. Both of their parents had died, and they were living with their grandmother, who was sick and concerned about who would care for her grandchildren when she died. As the camera panned to the grandmother, my tears started to flow. I couldn't imagine the pain she was feeling - the personal sacrifice she was making for these children.

The interviewer asked them questions about their favorite foods, what they liked to do in their free time, what grade they were in at school, etc. The girl was particularly shy, and her older brother prompted her several times. At the end, the worker asked if they knew any songs. In English, they sang a "Good Morning" song, complete with motions. It was adorable. Their names were Wendemagegn and Beza. He was eight, she was five.

The second sibling group was an 8-year-old boy and 7-year-old girl who were living in an orphanage. They had huge, genuine smiles on their faces and were giggling. They did the same thing, answering questions, singing their ABC's, etc. Their voices were beautiful.

I watched a few more interviews out of curiousity, mostly older children, and Mark came in to tell me that he was going to bed. I told him he had to see the two video interviews.

My timing wasn't really the best because he was really tired. When we finished, he didn't say much, and I didn't really know what he was thinking as he headed upstairs.

I went to bed that night, praying that God would watch over the sibling groups and find them families, even if it wasn't us. I asked God to show us if He wanted us to adopt one of the sibling sets.

In the weeks after our first adoption conversation and the return from our cruise, we continued to pray for wisdom. The decision seemed so overwhelming that I ended up just pleading for a neon sign from God. I told Him I'd do whatever He wanted, even if it meant NOT adopting, but I JUST NEEDED TO KNOW.

In the days after viewing the DVD, I continued to think about those four children. It seemed my thoughts would turn to them, especially as I drove, and I would spend time praying for them. I laugh now, remembering that in those first days I couldn't really remember how to pronounce Wendemagegn's name (Wind-a-mog-in). So my prayer was something like, "Dear God, be with Beza and, um, Wen..., um, whatever his name is."

After a day or two of that, I stuck the DVD back in so I could implant his name on my brain. Of course, watching it made me cry again.

More and more, my thoughts turned to Wendemagegn and Beza rather than the other sibling set.

- - - - - - - - - -

Referral Photos

Wendemagegn, 8   Beza, 6

On Friday, December 6th, a rare rainy day in Phoenix, I
was running errands during lunch. Like the last few days,
I spent the quiet time thinking about Wendemagegn and
Beza. Finally I said, "God, do you want us to adopt these
kids?"

Clear as a bell, I heard a "Yes." Not audibly, but it
was there - quick on the heels of my question. I had never
experienced an answer from God that way before. It was
amazingly beautiful and thrilling at the same time.

But quickly the doubts began to sink in. I have an over-
active imagination, and I can create whole "movies" in my
head, imagining how a situation will turn out. What if my
imagination just conjured up the answer I wanted to hear?
I mean, I'd never heard God answer me like that; so what
if it wasn't real?

Fortunately, God knows about my thick skull; so he
spoke to me again - just on a different topic. That afternoon
I picked up Natalie from preschool and headed home. I
took my normal freeway exit and sat in the left lane, ready

to turn. I glanced over and on the right side, pulled off the road, sat a pickup truck with two older men in the bed holding a sign that said "Out of gas, please help."

In the same way I had heard the "yes" earlier, I felt God tell me to give them $20. The light turned green and, somewhat annoyed, I changed lanes and turned right at the corner. It's a fairly rural area, but there is a gas station on that corner; so I pulled in there. Then I realized that a four-foot chain link fence and about 30 yards of overgrown grass separated me from the men. Plus it was still raining.

"Forget it. This is ridiculous," I said to myself, and I kept driving, swinging through the gas station and back onto the road, heading home.

But the internal battle waged, and I heard God tell me to help them. I had driven probably 100 yards when I u-turned and headed back - still slightly annoyed I might add. This was really inconvenient after all.

Five-year-old Natalie piped up from the back, "Mommy, WHAT are you doing?" She clearly thought I was crazy, or lost.

I was still arguing with God as I pulled into the gas station, circled around the pumps again and finally pulled up along the fence. I got out in the rain and headed toward the men.

One of them jogged to the fence where I stood. I handed him the $20 bill with a half-hearted (because I was still annoyed) "God bless" and got in the van - my heart racing.

Despite my reluctance and my internal war, I knew as I drove home that God had issued that directive for one reason - to show me that the "Yes" I heard earlier WAS from Him after all.

There was no denying it after that. God meant those two beautiful children from Ethiopia for our family.

That night, through many tears, I shared my day's experience with Mark. I think I still hoped that God had given him some equally-obvious sign as confirmation because the doubts kept arriving. I asked him if he'd "heard" from God that day. He said he hadn't, but maybe God was using ME to answer his questions as well.

Throughout the adoption process, and even in our time since the kids have been home, my roadside experience has served as a great comfort to me. I know, without a shadow of a doubt, that God called us to adopt those two kids into our family.

- - - - - - - - - -

That weekend couldn't pass fast enough.

I spoke to the director of the non-profit organization on Monday morning, and she was thrilled. She said she knew that Wendemagegn and Beza would find a great home fast. She explained the process and gave me information on the adoption agency with which they worked. There was so much to do - fingerprints, home study, references - paperwork galore.

The adoption agency couldn't officially match us with the kids until our home study was approved, but they would "unofficially" hold them for us as soon as our application was complete. (Sort of sounds like you're putting a sweater on layaway at the mall, doesn't it?)

With our adoption agency selected, we began to crunch the numbers. We estimated that by the time we were home with the kids, the adoption would cost us between $25,000-30,000. Yikes!

That's a LOT of money! No doubt it was worth it; it was just a question of where we were going to get it.

Fortunately, we had been paying a little over $2,000 toward our house payment every month the previous two and a half years. So we knew we had that money to use. At the time, we estimated that we could complete the adoption in six months. You can do the math and see that we still didn't have enough to cover the cost.

We had our savings - our $10,000 "emergency fund". It wasn't really designed for adoption, but we were perfectly willing to put that money toward the costs. We also knew that car repairs and other things were inevitable, and we would still be short of the total we needed.

Through my research, I knew there were grants available. But, I was afraid we wouldn't qualify because of our income and being debt free. I also knew that there were several avenues to get interest-free adoption loans.

We discussed this one night. Or rather, I said something like, "Well, I guess if we have to do one of those interest-free loans, we will; then we'll just pay it off as quickly as we can."

Neither one of us was completely happy with that idea. We committed eight years earlier to never go into debt again. Though this seemed a "worthy cause," we didn't feel much peace about it.

3
Debt, Dreams & Dependence

In January 2008, I went to Pittsburgh to visit my best friend, Kristen. One night while flipping through channels, I came across Dave Ramsey's new television show on Fox Business - a channel we didn't get at home.

It was a call-in show, very similar to his radio program. At this point, I can pretty much predict Dave's answers to most questions. "Sell the car!" "Get a second job!" I settled in to watch anyway.

That night a man called and explained that he really felt God calling him to a career change, which meant going to chiropractic school and incurring quite a bit of student loan debt. Of course I knew Dave wasn't going to support THAT idea! He encouraged the man to find creative ways to finance his schooling or wait and save up the money.

Then Dave uttered the words that rocked my world.

"There is not one example in the Bible of God calling someone to do something and then using debt as a tool to accomplish it!"

I think my jaw dropped into my lap. I had such little faith. Sure, I knew God could provide the means for us to adopt. But here I was, trying to take control and figure out HOW he would provide. I had put God in an itty-bitty box and forgotten how powerful He truly is.

Mark and I knew all the scriptural warnings about debt. God knew about our commitment to live debt free. So why would He ask us to adopt and then make debt part of that process?

The simple answer is, He wouldn't.

When I told Mark what I had heard, he said, "Well, I've been thinking the same thing, but I was afraid you'd be upset if I told you." And he was probably right.

However, we knew another big financial change was on the horizon, and adopting without going into debt would become even more challenging.

- - - - - - - - - - -

Brewing in the background for some time, Mark felt that his job with the church was not really where God wanted him to be. While he loved the staff he worked with, he felt more and more that he wasn't using the spiritual gifts and talents God had given him. He felt like God had something different in store for him in the area of missions.

We had spent months praying through the situation, asking God to guide Mark toward what he was supposed to be doing. Yet no obvious opportunities presented themselves. He just kept hearing, "Go".

So we took one of the biggest leaps of faith for us, and

Mark resigned from his position just a few weeks later.

Six months earlier, I had returned to work part-time as a graphic designer for our church. Just a few weeks before Mark resigned, I was offered a full-time position as communications director. So as Mark stepped away, I stepped into a full-time role that provided benefits and a salary.

But the salary was a little less than half of what Mark had earned. That "extra" $2,000 a month we had hoped to have without a house payment was gone. We could pay the bills and save a couple hundred dollars each month, but suddenly our adoption costs presented a whole new set of obstacles.

We were incredibly grateful to even be in the position where Mark could leave his job. If we had not been debt free, that decision would have been so much harder. Ultimately, I hope we would have obeyed God just the same, but I know we would probably have hesitated a lot more.

Our debt-free adoption commitment was going to take God-sized miracles. Yet we remained steadfast in our determination.

EATING, ENTERTAINMENT & EXTRAS

The Money You Already Have

4
Bucks, Budgets & Basics

When faced with a large obstacle, like an expensive adoption bill, taking the first step is the hardest.

Where do you start?

The best place is with the money you already have.

I know that "budget" can seem like a really scary and depressing word. Trust me; I felt the same way eight years earlier. It was overwhelming, and our budget never seemed to work for very long.

But as we learned from experience, if you don't have a budget, you are "leaking" money; money that can go toward your adoption.

So stop thinking of a budget as a restrictive, fun-killing necessity. Instead, think of it as a simple plan that tells your money where to go.

There's not room in the confines of this book to thoroughly explain how to create a household budget, but I have added a sample budget in the Appendix and on the book's website.

Besides, you don't need me to teach you about

budgets; you need Dave Ramsey's book, "Total Money Makeover." The book covers not only budgeting but also eliminating debt, saving, investing and more. (I also highly recommend Financial Peace University, a 13-week class that expands on the book material in an environment that provides personal support and encouragement.)

If this is your first time to use a budget, know that it will take you a couple months to fine tune it. Many people have no idea how much money to budget for things like groceries and clothing. Save all your receipts during these months; this will help you see what you're spending.

Early on (pre-Dave Ramsey), we mistakenly tried to create a generic monthly budget that worked all the time. But life isn't the same from month to month, is it? One month it is back-to-school shopping, the next it's birthday parties. Each month is unique and so your spending plan must vary accordingly.

5
Coupons, Cable & Cars

Besides the monthly reviews of our budget, each time our family income changes (up or down), we reassess and adjust it accordingly. On the one hand, it was nice that we were already used to living on a pretty lean budget. On the other hand, this change meant we couldn't squeeze out a lot of extra money for our adoption.

We still found ways to save money by cutting back more on entertainment and eating out. I also knew I'd had my last pedicure, a rare treat anyway, for a LONG time. Whenever I was tempted to pick up some new item of clothing or DVD, those two beautiful faces would flash before my eyes and the item would go back on the shelf. I knew every penny counted.

Once you've established your household budget, take a long hard look to see where you can cut expenses and find more money for your adoption.

From our own personal experience and from working with dozens of couples while teaching Financial Peace University (FPU), the following areas seem to be the top categories to trim and reap the most reward.

- - - - - - - - - -

Eating Out

The average American household spends nearly $225
a month eating away from home. Brown bagging your
lunch might not be as much fun as eating out with your
co-workers, but the savings add up quickly. Pack leftovers
from last night's dinner or take a frozen entree instead.
Budget to eat lunch out maybe once a week or every other
week instead of every day.

Look at how often your family eats out and when.
If your family is like mine, eating out was occasionally
planned, but more often than not, it was a last resort. As in
"I can't think what to make for dinner" or "I'm too tired to
make something."

Now I make sure that we always have a couple of
frozen pizzas in the freezer, as well as some of those easy
family skillet meals. I don't suggest making those the
majority of your grocery list because that's expensive too.
But if a $7 pasta meal will save you from a $45 restaurant
bill, it's worth it. My kids also love when I make breakfast
for dinner - eggs and pancakes are always a hit and I
always have the ingredients on hand.

I've also been known to declare "fend for yourself"
night and everyone just eats whatever they want -
leftovers, cereal, or PB&J.

Before we started the adoption process, we had already
cut down on our eating out. We usually took the kids to

the local pizza and game place about once a month ($30) and then maybe two or three fast food stops each month. I'm going to age myself here, but I remember growing up when our family of five could eat at McDonald's for about $12. Today that number is closer to $30. That still adds up to about $100 a month.

We cut our pizza nights to once every other month and had more family movie nights at home with a rented DVD and frozen pizza, or "make your own pizza" night. The kids loved it just as much. Our budget loved it more.

I also kept a bag of snacks in the car to help stave off the hunger that often drove us to the fast food places in desperation. On the occasions when we went through a drive-thru, we learned to eat off the value menu, drink water and, to the despair of my kids, we stopped ordering the kids meal. (You know you just throw away the toy two weeks later when they're not looking!)

Possible Monthly Savings: $175

- - - - - - - - - -

Groceries
The US Department of Labor estimates that the average American family of four spends roughly $700 a month on groceries. How do you compare?

What if I told you that you could feed that same family of four on $75 a WEEK - less than half the national average? That's up to $400 a month for adoption expenses!

Now that we have four kids at home, I spend about

$100-$125 a week on groceries. (When I say "groceries," I am also including cleaning supplies, paper goods and basic toiletries.) Mary Ostyn, author of "Family Feasts for $75 a Week" and an adoptive mom, has seven kids living at home and feeds their family of nine for approximately $800 a month. (Her book is a great resource to learn more about saving on groceries. Plus it has **wonderful** recipes.)

So, how do I do it? I'll give you the basics. It comes down to three things: planning, weekly sales, and coupons.

Planning: The key to sticking to a grocery budget (and avoiding the "nothing-to-eat-so-we'll-go-out" quandary) is a menu plan. A day or two before payday, I prepare a meal plan for that pay period. I include main dishes, side items and a dessert if needed (which is not very often). I make my menu with my calendar open so I can see what nights we will be gone, what nights dad will be gone (which means I make something really easy like grilled cheese sandwiches), and what days we have after-school activities and limited meal prep time. On those nights, I use the slow cooker or make an easy freezer meal.

After planning my menu, I check my pantry to see if I have the ingredients for each meal. I add anything I am missing to my grocery list. My goal is to make two large shopping trips each month and no more than two quick trips for stuff like milk and bread.

I've invested a bit of time to create a list of "standard" meals that I make for our family for easy reference. As I try new recipes and find successful ones, I add them to the list. If you can find 30-40 meals your family likes, put them on an easy rotation system.

Several companies exist that will help you with your meal planning. E-mealz (www.e-mealz.com) is a subscription service that, for $5 per month, provides weekly meal plans based on grocery store sales for a variety of stores. The weekly menus include recipes, instructions and a grocery shopping list that has an average weekly cost of $75. They provide plans for special diets like gluten-free and low carb, too.

Weekly Sales: Your local grocery store most likely has weekly sales. Ours seem to cycle on a Wednesday - Tuesday pattern, and the new ads arrive in the Wednesday paper or in the mail. If you don't get copies of your store circulars, you can find them online.

As I'm menu planning, I look at what's on sale, particularly in the meat department. If chicken is on sale, it's very likely we'll be eating lots of chicken-based dishes. I also watch the fruit and produce deals. Over time, I have come up with my "maximum spend" list. For example, I will not pay more than $1 per pound for apples. If I can't buy them for that or less, then I don't buy any. (Frequently, they are as cheap as 33 cents a pound.) We eat apples and bananas pretty much year round and then add whatever fruit is seasonal and on sale.

I have the luxury of a chest freezer in the garage, which has proved invaluable. (We purchased it used about six years ago for $150.) When meat or poultry goes on sale for a really great price (like boneless, skinless chicken breasts for $1.57/lb), I stock up. Depending on my grocery budget that month, I might buy four packages, or I might buy eight.

Then in my next menu planning cycle, I know I have chicken, and I add some chicken dishes to the menu. That saves me money on that week's groceries that I can use to stock up on another item on sale at a really good price.

Now, if you're like me, when someone mentions shopping multiple stores to take advantage of all the sales, my eyes glaze over. Because, you know, I have all that spare time - NOT.

But did you know that Walmart will match their competitor's prices? That means if apples are on sale for 34 cents a pound at one store, milk for $1.49 at another and you're going to Walmart for other items, you only need to make ONE trip. Take the competitor's ads with you and when the cashier gets to the sale item just say "That is price matched at $1.49." Sometimes they ask to see the ad, but most cashiers familiarize themselves with the weekly ads. I've even had a couple of cashiers tell me a better price than the one I knew about!

(To help the cashier, and myself, I try to group all my price-matched items in one area of the shopping cart and then load them on the belt at the end of my order. The people in line behind you will thank you too.)

Coupons: When it comes to coupons there tend to be three groups of people - those that hate them, those that use them occasionally, and the fanatics (and I mean that lovingly). There are tons of websites, blogs and subscription services that will show you how to save

HUNDREDS of dollars on groceries every month.

I've included some great web sites in the Appendix. I will summarize it this way: by combining coupons, weekly sales and store coupon policies (like doubling, tripling, etc.) it is possible for you to get $175 in groceries for $30. Yes, I said $30. Now that $30 worth of groceries won't necessarily go together to make a meal. But, by stockpiling sale items you will save money in future months. I've been known to come home with 20 boxes of cereal when I can get it for 49 cents a box.

Before our adoption, I would have put myself in the second category. I'd clip coupons sometimes, and save a few bucks here and there. But for the most part, I didn't bother.

My husband, however, LOVES a good bargain - and the hunt for a good bargain. Apparently, he had too much time on his hands during 10 months of unemployment. He stumbled upon one of the websites that explained how to save tons of money at Walgreens and CVS. Next thing I knew, our linen closet had enough shampoo, conditioner, body wash, razors, deodorant, toothpaste, toothbrushes, cough syrup, facial wash and air freshener to last us a year. Wait! It's been two years and we still have stuff left - probably enough to last us ANOTHER two years. In all, I would say that he spent around $50-$75 for what is easily $400-$500 worth of toiletries.

Granted, he spent a lot of time pursuing those bargains, and I'm not suggesting you go that far. But the possibilities exist.

A note about bulk shopping...

I know a lot of people who talk about saving money mention buying in bulk at warehouse stores. But if you're not careful, you can walk out having spent your weekly grocery money and not be able to make a single meal out of what's in your grocery cart.

I've learned that just because it's in bulk doesn't necessarily mean it's cheaper - especially when you take into consideration discounts after coupons. We have a few grocery items that I regularly buy at warehouse stores - milk, chicken nuggets, hamburger patties, frozen pizza, ketchup (my kids put it on everything) and baby carrots. Everything else I buy at regular stores on sale or with coupons.

Possible Monthly Savings: $400

- - - - - - - - - -

Entertainment & Media Services

When we started our adoption, we cut back our satellite TV package and saved about $30 a month. About a year ago (long after the kids were home), we realized that we hardly watched anything on the satellite channels. We had limited our kids TV watching to the weekends, Mark rarely watches anything other than sports and most of my favorite shows are on network television.

Quite honestly, the thing I loved most about our satellite service was the digital video recorder. Now, thanks to the wonders of Hulu.com and the network websites, you can watch most TV shows online at your convenience.

Our $8 monthly Netflix subscription lets us stream a lot of great movies and popular kid's shows through our Wii. We don't even miss the satellite. (For you tech heads, check out things like Roku, PlayOn TV and some of the other streaming media avenues.)

The average family spends $75 a month on their cable or satellite package. In the course of 12-18 months that could be $900-$1,300 toward your adoption.

We've also learned to wait for a lot of movies to come out on video. Or we look for the theaters that offer "first matinee showing" tickets at $5. If you rent a ton of videos, look at Netflix. If you only rent newer releases, find a Redbox near you and rent them for $1.

It's hard, if not impossible, to imagine living without cell phones. But you can shop around and see if you can find a cheaper plan, possibly combining phones into a family program.

Four years ago our cell phone contract expired and we purposefully refrained from extending it. I admit, the allure of a free new phone is tempting. But instead, we've purchased new-to-us phones on eBay and maintained our flexibility. We recently switched to Walmart Family Mobile. We get unlimited talk and text plus all the data we need for email and web usage for about $45-50 per phone. The move saves us $100 a month. Other prepaid phones like Boost and Virgin Mobile are worth looking into as prices continue to drop.

A lot of families have already eliminated their home phone and just use their cell phones. I never wanted to do that when our kids were younger in case they needed to call 9-1-1. We talked about it again just a few months ago, but our kids are old enough now that their friends call the house. Our kids don't have cell phones (and won't for a while), and we didn't want their friends calling our cell phones, which are also our primary work phones.

With a little research, Mark found the perfect solution. Ooma is a voice over IP service without the monthly fee. We bought a refurbished Ooma Hub for $99. It plugs into the wireless internet router and then into our existing phone handset. We still have caller id, call waiting and voice mail, but we only pay taxes and government fees each month. Instead of $25 a month, we're spending $4. The box pays for itself in five months and then we get to enjoy the savings.

Possible Monthly Savings: $50-150

- - - - - - - - - -

Gifts

Gift-giving can get ridiculously expensive between family, friends and kids. Years ago, we decided, jointly with our families, to adjust the system.

Christmas: Each year, the adults draw names so they buy for one other adult. Typically, we spend about $40-50 for that gift. Then we buy for all the nieces and nephews.

Giving gifts to kids is way more fun anyway. We spend about $10-15 for each child and have occasionally pooled this money for a group gift they can all enjoy - like a new Wii game. We spend a little bit more on our kids, but we still don't go overboard - around $40 per child.

Some of you may spend even less, but for some that may seem like a drastic cut. You might even have teenage children who would stage a revolt. Odds are, especially if you're pursuing international adoption, your money values are beginning to shift as you realize the incredible wealth we have as Americans when compared to the rest of the world.

Along our journey, we began to educate Noah and Natalie to give them more global awareness. We found them incredibly receptive. They even surprised us sometimes with their generosity and sacrificing spirit.

Birthdays: My husband and I don't buy birthday gifts for our siblings anymore. Instead, we just send a heartfelt note. We still buy for our parents, because well, they deserve it! We buy for nieces and nephews, again spending $10-$15 each. (We have seven, so it still adds up.)

I have a couple of close friends who I like to celebrate birthdays with because they mean a lot to me. But usually that means taking them out to dinner and enjoying a night together (at least for those who live locally).

With four kids, it seems like someone is always coming home with a birthday party invitation. My daughter had five parties within the first six weeks of school this year. We finally realized we had to tell them that we might not go to all the parties. Obviously, they attend the birthday parties of their really close friends, but I can usually gauge how close they are by how much our kids talk about that child on a normal basis. Thankfully, it seems that as the kids get older there are fewer parties.

Again, our spending limit is about $10-$15. As I'm out shopping, I always keep an eye out for clearance toys and great prices on appropriate gifts. I buy them and put them away in a box in my closet. When we get a party invitation, we check the box before we make a trip to the store. I confess that I like this method mostly because it saves me from spending 30 minutes in the toy aisle while my child decides what to get the birthday kid.

I've had to absolve myself of some initial feelings of guilt because we don't spend as much on gifts as other families. But I realized most of that was self-imposed and out of some silly need to impress other parents. The birthday child certainly doesn't care as long as the gift is thoughtful and something they'll enjoy.

Speaking of birthday parties, we scaled back on how we celebrate our children's birthdays. On their birthday, they can invite two friends for a sleepover. Sometimes we'll go to Peter Piper Pizza, but most of the time we just make them a special birthday dinner, rent a movie and let them hang out and have fun with their friends. It's a lot less stress on me, and the kids enjoy it just as much. We'll do something special for the major milestones, like 13 & 16. As they get older I imagine the number of invited friends will increase as well.

Possible Monthly Savings: $25-$100

- - - - - - - - - -

The Impulse Buy

I also found that I saved a lot of money during our adoption process by just resisting the small impulse purchases - the cute $10 shirt, the newest Disney movie on DVD, the Starbucks drink, etc.

Possible Monthly Savings: Depends. How impulsive are you now?

- - - - - - - - - -

Bonus Category - Transportation

I'm going to throw a bonus category at you that may make you close the book and slam it on the coffee table. But hear me out.

Could you sell a car?

I'm not saying you should start riding public transportation, but look at how much money you spend on car payments each month. Based on the average car price and loan period in 2010, the average family has a car payment of $475 per month. That's PER vehicle - $950 per month for most families who own two cars.

When Mark and I first married, we just accepted car payments as a way of life. In the first four years, we owned six different vehicles, trading up every time and swallowing a larger car payment with every new car. When we decided to get out of debt, one of the first things we did was sell one of those cars. (The other one was almost paid off.)

Take a close look at your car payments. Could you sell one of those vehicles and buy a good quality used vehicle for $4,000-6,000 with lower payments? I promise they exist. In the 11 years since we started to pay off our debt, we've bought great vehicles with 60-70k miles for $3,000-$7,500.

Over the years of teaching Financial Peace University and doing financial counseling, Mark and I have talked to many people that think they are so upside down in their car loan that they could never sell it and get out from under the debt. I challenge you to pray about it. What seems impossible for man, is possible with God. As you look to make sacrifices to make your adoption possible, take steps of faith and trust God.

The Boulton family, of Southern California, turned in one leased vehicle, sold another car and bought two less expensive vehicles, allowing them to save hundreds of dollars every month. The dealership told them they would owe money on the leased car, but instead they received a check for $3,000. (That check, added to a just-completed fundraiser, gave them $50 more than they needed for their next agency fee.)

- - - - - - - - - - -

So, how much can you save per month? Multiply that

number by 12 to see the impact it will make over the course of your adoption process. Those with a longer process can save even more. Even on our already tight budget, I would estimate that we probably saved at least $2,500 - $3,000 during the year by cutting back expenses. That was enough for both kids' plane tickets home!

Once you've developed a budget and decided where you can save money, the key is to stick to it. Over the years, we have found that the best way for us to stick to our budget is to use cash. After I pay the regular bills (utilities, cell phone, insurance, mortgage, etc.), I determine our budgeted amounts for the rest of the items like groceries, entertainment, eating out, clothes and medicine. I withdraw that amount of cash on payday and put it in envelopes clearly labeled for each category.

When the money is gone, it's gone. When the kids pester you to order delivery pizza, you can look in your "eating out" envelope and see whether you can afford it.

Studies show that people spend 12-18 percent less when they use cash over plastic (even debit cards). So we try REALLY hard to use the debit card only for fuel. We're certainly not perfect, but I can tell you that on the months when we "fall off the wagon" we blow our budget every time.

Plain old white envelopes work or you can buy a envelope system wallet from daveramsey.com. There are also some cute handmade ones on Etsy.com.

FOCUS, FUNDRAISE & FULFILL

The Tools You Need

6
Search, Sort & Sell

Look around your house and your garage to see what you have that you don't use anymore, specifically the bigger items. Do you have exercise equipment that spends most of its time draped with clothes or old video game systems your kids no longer play? Gather them up and sell them – either on Craigslist or eBay. (Research prices on both to see which method works better. Obviously, sell items too big to ship on Craigslist.)

You might also consider things you use but are willing to sacrifice for the greater good of bringing a child into your family - the flat-screen TV, boat or recreational vehicles, timeshare, etc.

Next gather the smaller stuff. If you haven't used something in six months (12 on the outside), sell it! Start a pile in your garage and spend a little time each day sorting. You can clean out a closet in a couple of hours. Plus, you'll feel better when you've put everything away in a neat, organized fashion. Or maybe that's just me - I am a little obsessive-compulsive.

Even if it takes you a month, slowly go through the house and garage and build a pile. The goal is to sell all of it at a garage sale, which is covered in detail in Chapter 8.

A Note about eBay

Selling stuff on eBay does take time, but it is easy to do from home. All you need is a digital camera and shipping materials. If you plan on selling a large quantity of items, buy an inexpensive postage scale so that you can weigh packages at home and label them for shipping. This saves you time at the post office and allows you to just drop off the already-paid packages. If you've never used eBay before, the site shows you all the basics.

http://pages.ebay.com/sellerinformation/index.html

7
Babysitter, Barista & Barber

Over the years, I have taken freelance design jobs as an extra source of income. In the beginning, we used it to pay off debt; then we purchased luxuries like new furniture or extra vacations that weren't in our regular budget. I never advertised for clients, they came to me by word-of-mouth from friends, co-workers and family. Sometimes, I'd go months without any jobs, then have one or two, then nothing again for awhile.

A few weeks after Mark left his job, the freelance work trickled in and then it piled up! On several jobs, I earned more than $1,000-1,500, which we put into our adoption savings. This was a huge encouragement to us that indeed, God was faithful to our commitment.

Is there a way you could make additional income above what you make now? If you delivered pizzas a couple of nights a week, you could stash away $500-600 a month.

What about a newspaper route?

If you're a stay-at-home mom, could you provide

childcare for one or two additional kids? Check your state laws, but most states will allow you to care for a small number of children before you must become licensed. Depending upon your area, you could earn $100 or more each week per child for providing full-time care. Or maybe you could offer "mom's-day-out" babysitting once a week to other stay-at-home moms.

Some women decide to temporarily return to work to help pay adoption expenses. Jodie Clements was a stay-at-home mom to her three kids before she and her husband Carl began their Ethiopian adoption process. She returned to work full-time as an elementary school counselor. After childcare expenses, they saved three quarters of her salary for their adoption, and Daniel came home in November 2008. After a brief leave of absence, Jodi finished out the school year before she resumed stay-at-home mom duties.

The Clements Family - RuthAnn, Carl, Daniel, JohnMark, Jodie & Abigail

Lori Stewart* took a 20-hour-per-week job at Starbucks - not only for the extra income, but because Starbucks

*Name changed for privacy

offers an adoption assistance program. Starbucks currently offers qualified employees reimbursement of up to $4,000 for adoption expenses, as well as two weeks paid time off for travel and homecoming adjustment. The Stewarts received a $3,000 grant. Lori worked for a short time after they brought their son home before giving her notice. (For a list of other companies that provide adoption reimbursements, see the Appendix.)

My friend, Jen, is a hair stylist. She held a couple hair-cutting events and asked people to donate to their tax-deductible grant fund. They received $800 in donations.

The Sloniger Kids - Aurora, Ally, Jonas, Rienne & Abram

I would stress that you and your spouse, if you're married, must agree on this issue. Taking on additional work at the expense of your marriage or your family is not worth the money.

So, we had some savings, we trimmed the budget even more and we had some extra income.

Now it was time to get creative.

- - - - - - - - - -

After you re-examine your budget and apply for grants (see Chapter 11), the gap between your funds and adoption costs is the perfect opportunity for creative fundraising. Before you proceed, check with your adoption agency about any rules they, or your adoptive country, may have about fundraising.

There are endless possibilities. Obviously, you won't want to do every idea mentioned. But find a few that sound fun and that you can do within the limits of your schedule. Some ideas might work best with co-workers, some with family and some with your community. It's about finding the right idea(s) for each of them.

The next three chapters cover three areas of fundraising - events, sales and online.

- - - - - - - - - -

8
Rummage, Raffle & Run

Events That Raise Money

Event fundraisers are as old as time. I imagine we've all participated in a car wash or two at some point or sold candy bars for school and club activities. You can adapt many, if not all, of these same ideas for your adoption fund.

- - - - - - - - - -

Garage Sales

Garage sales have one of the biggest return potentials in the shortest amount of time, and you can do them multiple times.

I am always purging closets of toys, clothes and junk. Most often, it goes to the thrift store in small batches. But at the beginning of our adoption, we'd built up quite a pile in the garage, and so we opted for a garage sale - something we do every couple of years. We joined forces with our friends, the Slonigers, who were 10 months into their adoption process, and another adoptive family, the Bruyns. We knew we'd not only collect more stuff, but we'd have a lot more fun with friends.

First, pick a date for the sale. Give yourself at LEAST six to eight weeks to plan and collect donations. Avoid holiday weekends because many people are out of town or have family plans. Consider having a two or three day sale - Friday/Saturday sales are popular in our town, and, surprisingly, we made the majority of our money on Friday.

I designed a simple flyer on the computer and sent it via email to all our friends, asking for donations to help us raise funds. We listed multiple drop off locations (our three homes and a work location) and offered to pick up items if necessary. If you don't have a large vehicle, see if a friend will help pickup furniture and other large items. (See the Appendix for a flyer example.)

While you're advertising for donations, solicit volunteers to help with day-before preparations and sale-day support. Keep a list of people that offer to help so you can call them when it's time.

Ask your friends to tell their friends. Spread the word on your blog, Facebook and Twitter. We received stuff from people we didn't know who heard about it from mutual friends.

At the end of six weeks, the donations filled up two bays of our garage, a storage room, a carport and the back patio of the Sloniger's house. We had larger items like beds, dining room tables, and mattresses, but the majority

Garage sale collections at ONE of our locations.

of it was smaller items - clothes, toys, books, small electronics and tools. You name it, we had it!

Check with friends for folding tables you can borrow for sale day. If you belong to a church, they might loan them to you. You can always rent them, but free is better. To display items, we used six six-foot tables plus the surfaces of some of the furniture we were selling.

Because the majority of the stuff was at the Sloniger's house and they live in a high-traffic area, we had the garage sale at their house in late March.

All day Thursday, we arranged and priced stuff with the help of a couple of friends. Don't price stuff too high, but don't go too low either. Generally, you'll sell stuff for less than half of the retail price. Make the prices easy to add. We priced everything in 25-cent increments.

If you're wavering on a price, go with the higher amount because people will likely bargain, and then you can lower your price. Batch price some categories that have a large number of items. For example, sell all videos for 50 cents, all books for $1. Mark the category price on a sign by the items (grouped together), and keep a list of those categories and prices for the cashier's reference.

Our pile of donations included at least 15 lawn-size garbage bags full of clothes - totally overwhelming. We sorted through them and grouped them by baby, kid's, men's and women's. The high-end, name-brand items we pulled out, priced separately and hung on a clothes rack. On the day of the sale, we laid plastic tarps in the yard and put the clothes in the sorted piles. We priced everything at 50 cents each OR let shoppers fill an 8-gallon trash bag for $5. Our main goal was to sell as many clothes as possible. Don't bother folding clothing - it will be undone within the first 30 minutes.

Create signs on bright-colored poster board for the neighborhood and cover all the major nearby intersections with detailed signs - e.g., "HUGE GARAGE SALE Fri/

Sat 6 am - 12 noon" and an arrow. Using the same color poster board, put smaller arrow-only signs to guide shoppers through the neighborhood to your house.

The day before your sale, put a garage sale ad on Craigslist with a detailed list of some of the

The older kids, like Rienne Sloniger, took a turn as cashier.

larger furniture and electronic items.

Recruit help for the day of the sale - preferably friends with garage sale and negotiating experience. Arm everyone with a black marker. Set up one cashier station with a table and cash box. If a customer negotiates a better price on an item with one of your helpers, instruct your helpers to cross off the price and write the new one on the tag.

Make a big sign that says "Adoption Fundraiser." People haggle less when they realize the money goes to a good cause. Some even gave us extra money. Plus, we shared our adoption story with lots of people. If you already have a referral picture, put a copy by the cashier or on a poster.

You can make a few extra dollars by selling drinks, such as coffee, water or soda. Plus, it's a great way to involve kids. Some people have sold donuts and various baked goods, but check your local food handling code. Some states have exemptions for small-scale events for non-profits and schools that may include your function.

We sold a TON of stuff that first weekend, but we had so much left over at the end of Saturday that we had another sale at our house the following weekend. Even then, we didn't sell all of it. Instead of hanging on to it for another weekend, we passed everything on to a friend hosting her own garage sale a few weeks later. If you have room to store the leftovers, hang on to them and have another sale in a few months.

If you have big ticket items like furniture left over, list them on Craigslist. Make arrangements ahead of time with a local charity to pickup your smaller unsold items.

If you can't have garage sales in your neighborhood due to homeowner association rules or city restrictions, see if you can hold it in the parking lot of the local school or a church.

How much can you make? Depending on the scale of your sale, you can make a few hundred to a few thousand dollars. In four days, we made $5,200. It was exhausting, but fun and well worth the effort.

 Amount Raised: $5,200

Other Garage Sale Successes

More than 30 families donated items to the Hendricks family of Minneapolis for their garage sale. Kevin & Abby told shoppers they were adopting and, instead of pricing each item, asked people to give them a donation. They accepted most reasonable offers and found many people gave more than they would have normally paid. (They did, however, reject the 50 cent offer for the couch.)

The Hendricks had so much stuff that the garage sale lasted three weekends. By the third weekend, they marked EVERYTHING down to 25 cents. They still took three van loads to Goodwill, but they pocketed over $3,000 for their adoption.

 Amount Raised: $3,000

The Hendricks Family - Abby, Milo, Kevin & Lexi

The Crosby family specifically asked for only large items and kid's clothes. Linda took the nicest kid's clothes to the bi-annual kid's consignment sale and made $200. The rest she put in the garage sale, priced at $1. She listed several large items on Craigslist before the garage sale, making $650.

 Amount Raised: $2,000

The Oberhauser family of Chatham, Ill., advertised their two yard sales on the internet, in newspapers and on Christian radio. Flyers described their adoption of two-year-old Isaac from the Ukraine, and many shoppers made donations above their purchase amount.

 Amount Raised: $4,000

The Buoniconti family collected donations for five months before having two yard sales - one in June and one in August. Their kids sold lemonade, and Frank made fresh bread to sell.

 Amount Raised: $2,100

- - - - - - - - - -

5k Fun Run/Walk

Nicole & Chris O'Meara raised $5,000 with their 5k "Show Love Fun Run." The O'Mearas and six friends from church spent three months planning the event.

The 125 runners that participated paid a registration fee of $40 per person (or $80 per family), which included a T-shirt, on-course support and snacks after the race.

The O'Mearas advertised the Fun Run through community calendars, flyers around the planned run course and posters at all the coffee shops within a five-mile radius. They also used Facebook, Twitter and their church bulletin to promote the event. Local running clubs were notified via www.active.com.

The day included other activities for the 200 people who attended - coffee and pastries, a photo booth,

The O'Meara Family - Chris, Nicole & Joshua

cotton candy, balloon artists, face painting and a huge bounce house for the kids. Six local business sponsors covered the cost of these activities, as well as permits and event insurance.

A month before the run, the O'Mearas announced more than a dozen giveaway items and pre-sold raffle tickets for $1. As word got out, they received additional items for the raffle and had more than 30 items by race day. They sold 2,100 raffle tickets, mostly on the day of the run.

The giveaways included an adoption quilt, handmade pottery, sports tickets, ski lift tickets, a massage, photography session, iPod Nano, autographed music CDs, gift certificates for jewelry, haircuts, auto detailing, restaurants and more. The O'Mearas used traveler points to get the two iPods, but everything else was donated.

Nicole said next time she would use the more expensive items, like the iPods, in a silent auction instead of including them in the giveaway.

Not only did the fun run raise money, but the O'Mearas educated others about adoption by setting up an information table and placing various orphan and adoption facts along the course. Two families that attended are now considering adoption!

The 5k was so much fun that the O'Mearas plan to make it a yearly event and use the money to help other adopting families. They said they will target more running clubs, possibly even offering them a discount on registration. Since the park where the run was held allowed pets on leashes, they plan to do a better job of advertising at pet stores, groomers and kennels.

A survey at the Fun Run showed them that word of mouth accounted for more than half of the attendance.

$ Amount Raised $5,000

- - - - - - - - - -

Movie Night & Silent Auction

The Boulton family of Southern California held a movie night and silent auction fundraiser at their church to help fund their adoption of a toddler from Ethiopia.

They showed a family-friendly movie on a large screen in the church gym, and asked for a $10 donation per family. About 20 families attended and brought their own camp chairs and blankets.

Friends got involved and organized a corresponding bake sale and silent auction. The bake sale coordinator made sure that the donated cakes and cookies covered a variety of flavors and arranged everything during the sale. Church small groups and friends donated themed baskets, goods and services for the silent auction. The auction included a wide range of items so that even those that couldn't spend a lot, could still find something on which to bid.

Auction items included movie-themed baskets, handmade items, gift cards, a "date night" basket and

The Boulton Family - Autumn, Austin, Asher, Lyndsay, Bart & Aidan

tickets to a Lakers game and an NFL game. One friend created a "Trunk of Love" full of clothes and items for the Boulton's soon-to-be adopted daughter. The winner gave the trunk to Boultons as a gift. The trunk sold for $150!

The Boultons advertised the event on their blog and with flyers. (For more on silent auctions, see page 71.)

$ Amount Raised: $3,000

NOTE: Please be aware of copyright issues for these types of events. Even if you don't charge admission and instead ask for a "suggested donation," public viewing of a film requires special permission. You will need to obtain permission from either the copyright holder, the distributor or one of the film industry licensing companies. Many times if you let them know it is a one-time event to raise money for charity, they will give you permission. Do a Google search for "public performance rights movies" for more information.

- - - - - - - - - -

Both Hands Widow/Orphan Project

Several times the Bible lists orphans and widows together and commands us to care for both. The Both Hands Foundation creates a way for you to do just that - care for a widow and fundraise for your adoption of an orphan.

While Both Hands requires a grant application and approval (see page 117), I've included it here because it is also event-driven.

Years ago, founder JT Olson asked a friend to sponsor him in a golf tournament to raise funds for women in crisis pregnancies. The friend wrote back and said he'd gladly support his efforts if JT was working on a widow's house instead of playing golf.

Five years later, a different friend was adopting four children from Moldova and needed to raise funds for their expenses. JT remembered the letter, and the idea for Both Hands was born.

Once approved for a Both Hands/Lifesong grant, adoptive families recruit volunteers to help them for a one-day work project on the home of a widow. A minimum of 10 volunteers is needed, but the more you have, the better.

Each volunteer, along with the adoptive family, sends out a fundraising letter to their circle of friends and family, explaining the project and a bit about your adoption.

Next, the adoptive family partners with a widow who needs help around her home - painting, landscaping, cleaning, etc. Local churches and community service organizations like Meals on Wheels can help you find someone to help.

Once you determine the type of work your team will be doing, contact local businesses and ask if they will donate supplies. Paint is one of the easiest things to get donated.

On work day, have fun and enjoy the opportunity to encourage the woman you're helping. Both Hands is sure to be a life-changing experience for everyone involved. *www.bothhandsfoundation.org*

"It gave me the opportunity to live out James 1:27 in a way

*that I hadn't before and should be doing always. I attend
church with this lady and never thought once about asking
her if she needed anything. She lives alone, her kids are far
away and she is missing the love of her life. We got to love
on her for a day and to help her clean her house; most of all
we gave her company, which she needed."*
- Susan Allee

$ Amount Raised: $1,000 - $27,000 (average of $10,000)

Tips for success:

- As a group, send a minimum of 600 letters.
  Families who do, usually raise at least $10,000.
- Find a widow who's house needs labor intensive -
  not material intensive - work. Great examples are
  painting, landscaping and clean up.
- Diversify the age of your team; it helps with
  fundraising as well as on work day.
- Do a video interview with the widow you'll be
  helping at the beginning of the process. It will help
  you cast vision and motivate your volunteers.

- - - - - - - - - -

Dinner

When you hear "benefit dinner," don't be intimidated. It doesn't have to be a black tie affair with prime rib.

Think about your circle of friends and family and gear your dinner toward them. If you're a casual, laid back bunch, do a BBQ or spaghetti dinner. One of my friends did a soup and bread night. She had a bunch of her friends cook different kinds of soup in slow cookers. They bought bread, bowls and spoons and charged $5 per person. Donated baked goods were sold for dessert. At the end of the night, they netted $5,000!

If your connections are used to black tie dinners and willing to pay a higher ticket price, then by all means, go for a more formal event.

Either way, a dinner will take some time to organize; so give yourselves at least two to three months to prepare. This is the perfect time to do a silent auction, which means you may want even more planning time. (See page 71.)

Here are some things to consider as you're planning:

VOLUNTEERS: You'll need people to help advertise, collect money, cook, serve, sell desserts and clean up. If you are including a silent auction, you'll need a set of several volunteers to work on collecting donations and organizing them. (See page 71.)

LOCATION: Ideally, find a location you can use free. It could be someone's backyard, a church or school multi-purpose room or an event hall. Make sure it has a nearby kitchen you can use.

FOOD: Whether you choose to do it yourself with

your volunteer team or have it catered, it never hurts to ask for donated items. As an alternative, you might find a few local business that are willing to sponsor the event. In exchange for some money to cover your costs, you can advertise for the business throughout the event. Drinks can be as simple as tea and lemonade. Instead of including dessert, consider getting friends to donate baked goods and sell them.

PROGRAM: Plan to have a program, even if it is brief. Take the time to share the story of why you are adopting and why you're raising funds. There are lots of great videos on the general topic of orphans that you could show. Again, depending on the crowd, you might include music or a guest speaker.

PRICE: Set your price according to the style of your event. Consider offering a "per family" price as well as an individual cost. This will encourage young families who have children and don't want to pay for a babysitter. Make a way for people to donate at a later point in the evening - a jar or basket by the dessert table for example. You could even do something fun like a money tree.

ACTIVITIES: As you read through this book, you may see other things, besides a silent auction, that would pair well with the dinner - movie night, karaoke or family pictures. If you are selling T-shirts, jewelry or coffee, put that out on a table. Depending on the location, see if you can get a bounce house donated or sponsored. Having kids occupied will free up their parents to look at auction items. (Find a teenager who can act as supervisor for the bounce house and limit how many children are inside at a time.)

GIVEAWAYS: Have a few fun giveaways during the night. Even if you're not doing a silent auction, see if friends or business will donate a few items - gift cards or certificates are perfect. Include a couple of your adoption T-shirts. You can manage the giveaways through a raffle ticket system (give each person a ticket as they pay) or do something like put numbers under the chairs.

ADVERTISING: Use every method you can think of. A website like www.evite.com makes email invitations and RSVPs easy. Set up an event on your Facebook page and invite all your friends. Ask them to share it with others they know. Promote it on your blog. Ask if you can place an announcement in the church bulletin or put up flyers. Ask to send a flyer home with the other students in your child's class.

Whatever you do, DON'T try to do it all yourself. Enlist all those people who have asked, "What can I do to help."

$ Amount Raised: $1,000-$10,000

Stephen & Dottie Story of Augusta, Ga., organized a catered banquet and asked invitees to choose the level of donation they wanted to give. Dan Cruver, director of Together for Adoption, spoke to the 75 people in attendance.

The Story Family - Stephen, Dottie, Elijah, & Evangeline

(The Storys gave Dan an honorarium and covered his travel expenses.)

$ Amount Raised: $10,000

- - - - - - - - - -

Silent Auction

A silent auction is the perfect fundraiser to pair with another event like a benefit concert, dinner or movie night. (It can also be done online - see page 112.)

Start soliciting donations a minimum of two to three months in advance. This is a great opportunity to use friends who have offered their time. (If they haven't offered, then ask anyway.) Put them to work getting donations for the auction.

Items can be goods or services (see examples on pages 74) and can come from companies, individuals or groups. Donations might be single items or a themed basket of goods.

If you belong to a church that has small groups, ask if you can contact the leaders and ask their group to put together a themed basket of goodies. This lets people help without a big expense. (See page 75-76 for basket theme ideas.) After you collect their basket, use shrink wrap or colored cellophane and some ribbon to package it nicely.

When soliciting for large items like electronics and appliances you may have better responses with independently-run stores. Instead of an outright donation, some might agree to give you the item at cost and not charge you until after the auction. (Make the minimum bid on the item equal to your cost.)

Make a master list of all the items collected for the auction; include the donor's name, their contact information and any cost to you. Include space to note who won the item, final price and if they have paid.

Recruit volunteers to help as judges, bankers and runners.

Auction Details

Using a small label, number each item to correspond with your master list.

Print a bid sheet for each item that details the item, its number, how much it is worth and who donated it. Include a minimum bid (approximately 25% of the retail value) and the minimum bid increment. A good guideline is: $1 for items up to $50, $2 if the item is worth $50-100 and $5 for items over $100. Add several lines with columns for the bidder's name, phone number and their bid amount.

If needed, make up a certificate for donated services that don't have a pre-made certificate. For small items like event tickets, you may want to print a certificate instead of displaying the actual tickets to prevent them from getting lost.

Place judges near the tables to ensure that bids are meeting the right increases, to answer questions and to monitor the donations. Have extra blank bid sheets available in case the first bid sheet fills up.

Tape the bid sheets down to the table in front of the item and secure a pen on a string near each sheet.

The Boulton family included a silent auction during their movie night.

Give people a warning when there are only 10-15 minutes left to bid. If there are items with no bids, be sure to promote those.

When the time is up, have the judges immediately pick up the bid sheets. Double-check them to be sure the bidding increased correctly.

Have the bankers sort the bid sheets by last name of the winner. If someone won multiple items, staple those sheets together and total the amount they owe.

Call auction winners to the bank table one or two at a time to pay for their items. While they are paying, have a runner go get the item from the tables. (If for some reason a winner does not want to pay for the item they won, move on to the next highest bidder.)

Not all winners will still be at the event; that is why you collected their phone number. In the day or two after the auction, call them and arrange for payment and pickup of their item. (If there are a lot of leftover items, ask one or two of your volunteers to help you make calls and get items delivered.)

Follow up with thank you notes to your donors and volunteers.

Examples

Goods
- Event tickets - sports, theater, ballet
- Memberships - fitness center, museum
- Trip/vacation packages or timeshare stays
- Electronics - computers, DVD players, iPod, video game players
- Appliances & furniture

Services
- Photography session
- Website design services
- Tax preparation
- Lessons - music, swimming, karate
- Auto - oil change, tire rotation and balance, detailing
- Birthday party packages - pizza parlors, kid gyms
- Dental - teeth whitening
- Home services - pest control, landscaping, pool care, painting, furnace/AC servicing
- Spa/pampering - hair styling, manicure/pedicure, massage, spa treatments

Themed-Basket Ideas

- Movie Night - DVDs, popcorn, candy, drinks, gift card to video rental store
- Date Night - restaurant or movie theater gift cards, candles, romantic music CD
- Gourmet Kitchen - spices, gadgets, cookbook
- Family Fun Night - board games, puzzles, DVDs, candy, music
- Wii (or other console) - extra remotes, video games, snacks, gaming guides
- Coffee - flavored coffee, coffee cups, travel mugs, gift card to coffee shop
- Baking - cookie cutters, pot holders, cookbooks, measuring cups, cookie mixes, frosting, sprinkles
- Pool Party - pool toys, sunscreen, beach towels, goggles
- Ice Cream - toppings, bowls, scoops, gift card to ice cream parlor
- Christmas - ornaments, wrapping paper, cards, decorations
- Disney - toys, games, movies
- Gardening - hand shovel, seeds, bulbs, watering can, hat, pots, gift card to garden center
- Do-It-Yourself - tools, how-to books, gift card to hardware store
- Spa - bath products, tub pillow, music CD, gift card for massage or pedicure
- Sports - game tickets, jersey, ball, hats, T-shirt

- Books (adult or child) - books, reading light, gift card to bookstore
- Chocolate Lovers - candy, gourmet chocolate, hot chocolate mix, gift card to candy shop
- Golf - balls, bag tag, towels, tees, golf gloves, gift card for 18 holes
- Babies - bibs, bottles, onesies, pacifiers, blankets, rattles, soft books
- Grill Master - BBQ tools, sauces, cookbooks, apron
- Camping - lantern, tin dish sets, hiking guides, trail mix, compass, pocket knife
- Car Care - auto wax, cleaners, tire gauge, car care books, steering wheel cover, chamois, sun shade
- Hobby Related - scrapbooking, sewing, model cars, jewelry making

$ Amount Raised: $1,000-$5,000+

- - - - - - - - - -

Karaoke Night

Kenny & Catherine Besk raised over $20,000 for their adoption with several different fundraisers, one of which is destined to provide lots of laughter along with donations.

A local family pub and grille in Santa Cruz agreed to donate space for the Besks to host a karaoke night.

The Besk Family - Kenny, Lucy, Catherine & Maizie

The karaoke service was offered at half price, and the pub owner offered to cover that cost as well.

Here's how karaoke night works:

- For $10 a person signs up a friend to sing AND picks the song they have to sing.
- When the friend's name is called, he can pay $5 to change the song OR add a friend to sing with him.
- Or for $15, he can get out of singing the song, and the person who signed him up has to sing it.
- Those who pay $30 when they arrive can get in, cheer and laugh, but are safe from having to sing all night.

With a fun group of friends, karaoke night is bound to be a blast!

$ Amount Raised: $1,311

- - - - - - - - - -

Concert

Benefit concerts are a great fundraising idea if you're connected with musicians and can put some time and energy into advertising. Combine a concert with a silent auction and sales of T-shirts or other similar items to maximize the opportunity.

If you attend church, ask your worship team if they would host a "Night of Worship" to benefit your adoption.

Take 10 minutes to share about the need of orphans and specifically your adoption journey. Whether you sell tickets or ask for donations at the door, make a way for people to give additional donations.

The Besk family took advantage of their art-centered community and talented friends by putting on a benefit concert. Two local bands, Dangle Root and Hurricane Roses, donated their time and one of the band members got the concert space donated. There was a suggested $10 donation at the door, and the Besks sold original concert posters painted by a friend.

 Amount Raised: $1,770

- - - - - - - - - - -

Restaurant Fundraisers

Many restaurants offer fundraising nights for non-profit organizations. If you are working with a 501(c)(3) grant organization (see page 115), you can use the following idea as well, with the funds going into your grant.

Restaurant fundraisers take very little work other than contacting the restaurant and advertising the event. Many chain restaurants offer fundraising nights, but each individual owner may operate differently. Some require your friends to bring in a pre-printed flyer when they dine; some just have customers tell the wait staff they came to support you. Fundraising nights are usually held on one of the least-busy weekday nights, and you receive a percentage of the sales from your referrals.

The list below features major chain restaurants, but many locally-owned restaurants will host fundraiser nights and may offer you a bigger percentage. When you contact a restaurant, here are some questions to ask:

- What percentage will our group receive? (Usually between 10-25 percent.)
- What days are available?
- What hours are available?
- Is it limited to just our referrals or will we receive a percentage from everyone who dines during the time period?
- Do takeout or drive-thru orders count?
- Can we set up an informational display and solicit general donations during the night? (If so, be sure the display features your non-profit grant organization and adds your personal story.)

You can raise anywhere from a few hundred dollars to over $1,000, but the good thing about restaurant fundraisers is that you can schedule several of them throughout your adoption process.

$ Amount Raised: $200-$1,000+

Restaurants

Applebees
(Flapjack Breakfast Fundraiser)
Arby's
Baja Fresh
Bennigan's
Big Boy
Black-Eyed Pea
Boston Market
Burger King
Carl Jr's
Chevy's Mexican Restaurants
Chick-fil-A
Chipotle
Chili's
CiCi's Pizza
Culvers
Fazoli's
Fresh Choice
Friendly's
Fuddruckers
Jack-in-the-Box
Jersey Mike's
KFC
La salsa Fresh Mexican Grill
Loco's Deli

Maggie Moo's
Max & Erma's
McAlister's Deli
McDonalds
Mongolian BBQ
O'Charley's
Outback Steakhouse
Panera Bread
Paradise Bakery (Currently AZ only)
Papa John's Pizza
Papa Murphy's
Pizza Hut
Pizzeria Uno
Ponderosa
Rio Bravo
Sonic
Steak & Ale
Sweet Tomatoes
Subway
Taco Cabana
Texas Roadhouse
Tortuga's
TRU
Wendy's
Wildflower Bread Company
Zany Brainy

Zumba Fitness Party

While not the biggest money raiser, Catherine Besk says their Zumba Fitness Fundraiser was one of her favorites. Zumba, one of the newest exercise trends, uses Latin-inspired dance in a fun high-energy fitness program. One of Catherine's friends, who is an instructor, donated her time and got her studio to agree to let them use the space for free. People paid $15 for the one-hour Zumba class and had a ton of fun.

 Amount raised: $275

The McKinney family
Tony, Michelle, Caleb & Mekhi

The McKinney family worked like crazy to fundraise the $25,000 they needed to adopt a little girl from Ethiopia. Their Zumba party was a BIG success! They started out with one instructor who then recruited two more friends so they could offer two 45-minute Zumba sessions. They pre-sold tickets (minimum donation of $10) through eventbrite.com and printed tickets that they gave their friends to sell. They even gave their friends some incentive and offered $100 cash prize to the person who sold the most tickets. (The winner ended up donating it back to the adoption fund.) They created a fun photo booth, played adoption videos, offered snacks and had a raffle drawing as well.

 Amount raised: $3,000

g Out of the Box

idea too crazy right? Think you'd be willing to shave your head?

Kevin Hendricks decided it was definitely worth it when he and his wife Abby were adopting their son Milo from Ethiopia. With hair down to his shoulders, he pledged to shave his head if he could raise $2,000 by his birthday. He mailed out letters to 250 of their friends to explain the idea and tell them about their adoption. Kevin included a FAQ sheet answering common adoption questions and explained why they needed to raise money.

On a full-color business card, he put a picture of himself with long hair on one side, and a Photoshopped picture of himself bald on the other side.

In the two months leading up to his birthday, 45 people donated to the project. On his birthday, Kevin videotaped the shaving, photographed his newly-shiny head and sent the picture, along with a thank you note, to each of the donors.

His hair-brained idea didn't seem so crazy when they added $4,500 to their adoption fund!

Kevin attributes the success to the amount of time and effort he spent crafting the letter and including the pictures. They chose not to use the internet for the project because of their adoption agencies advice about online fundraising.

Kevin had so much fun with the idea that he's done some additional hair-related fundraisers to raise money for clean water through Charity: Water.

$ Amount Raised: $4,500

Right before the head shave.   Bald head, $4,500 in adoption fund.

- - - - - - - - -

Blessed by Friends

One of the things I love hearing about, is the way friends and family rally around adoptive families, sometimes coming up with and implementing amazing fundraisers all on their own.

Sarah and Steve Carter of Southern California were blown away when their friends Tommy and Kendall asked wedding guests to give toward the Carter's adoption in lieu of gifts. Tommy and Kendall made a beautiful video that shared their heart and then allowed Sarah & Steve to share about their Ghana adoption journey. They sent the DVD to all their wedding guests along with a RSVP/ Donation card. (Guests could also give at the wedding.) Two months after their wedding, Tommy and Kendall presented the Carters with a check for $7,000 - a third of their needed adoption funds.

$ Amount Raised $7,000

The Carter Family - Steve, Emerson & Sarah

A couple of months before they were scheduled to head to Uganda to pick up their new son, Lara Dinsmore's blog was lovingly hijacked by her friends Shelly and Colleen who threw her a virtual baby shower. With the goal of funding the Dinsmores' plane tickets, Shelly and Colleen had gathered some great door prizes including a Canon EOS Rebel T3i camera, tshirts and gift certificates. They set a goal of raising $5,000 in a week and they did it!

$ Amount Raised: $5,000

More Ideas

Bingo - Bingo supplies are available at your local party store. Get some prizes donated and have a fun night with friends.

Bowling Tournament - Ask a local bowling alley to donate or give you a reduced price on lanes on a less busy night. Charge a registration fee for teams of four bowlers. Offer a great prize, preferably donated, to the winning team.

Car Wash - Put your kids to work, get their friends or your church youth group involved. Ask for donations.

Dance-a-thon - Pick a theme (50s, disco, etc.) and charge an entry fee. Find a DJ who will donate their time and get local businesses to sponsor prizes for Best Costume and Best Dance Moves. Sell baked goods. As an alternative participants could gather pledges for each half hour they dance and see who can dance the longest.

Skate-a-thon - Same as the dance-a-thon but hold it at the local ice skating or roller skating rink.

Golf Tournament - Work with a local golf course to coordinate a benefit golf tournament. Charge a per team entry fee. Ask local businesses to sponsor prizes or investigate "hole-in-one" prize insurance.

9
Clothes, Coffee & Crafts

Raising Money Through Sales

Seems that everyone who is adopting is selling something.
Why? Because it works and there are dozens of ideas.
You're only limited by your creativity.

Handmade Items

First, look at your existing talents. Do you paint?
Scrapbook? Make jewelry? Sew? Quilt? Hundreds of
adoptive families are earning money for their adoptions
by using their existing creative talents. There are several
avenues that can be used to sell handmade items - eBay,
your own blog or Etsy.com.

Before the Crosby's referral of a girl from China,
Linda's sister-in-law, Jennie, nicknamed her soon-to-be
niece "ZaZa". Jennie decided to put her sewing skills to
work and take advantage of her stash of fabric remnants
to create "Bags for ZaZa". Linda, her mother, Grace, and
Jennie's sister, Leah, and workmate, Jenn, joined the

sewing fun to create fun, funky, messenger bags and sell them online.

They placed ads on Craigslist and contacted local upholstery shops to solicit leftover material. This helped keep costs low as the bulk of their materials were donated.

They sold the bags online using a blog and a silent auction format. They listed each bag with several photos and a starting price of $25. People bid on the bag by writing their bid in the comments section. The average sales price was $40 with one bag selling for $150. Buyers then paid actual shipping costs.

Linda printed free business cards (www.vistaprint. com) and included several in each bag for advertising.

At the end of 18 months, Bags for ZaZa had raised $6,900. ZaZa turned out to be Nora, a beautiful girl who came home from Colombia in December 2010. *www.BagsForZaza.blogspot.com*

A ZaZa messenger bag

 Amount Raised: $6,900

Kelley Crance-Agnew and her husband are adopting a 6-year-old boy from Ethiopia. With three kids and two jobs, Kelley turned to crafting to make some extra money for their adoption. She discovered that not only did she love being creative, but it was a great way to spend time with her kids. Their 8-year-old learned to sew, and their

13-year-old now designs stuffed animals made out of old T-shirts.

Kelley's store features T-shirts, hats, beanies, onesies and bags with fabric African appliqués. In the first three months of sales, she made $450. Kelley's advice is to let EVERYONE know about your store by sharing it on your blog, Facebook and at other fundraisers. She has also donated items to other adoptive families who are hosting giveaways, which increased her traffic.

www.etsy.com/shop/PureeAway

 Amount Raised: $450

During the wait for their Ethiopian adoption referral, Laura Ducommun searched the stores for the perfect black doll. Disappointed in her options, she decided to create one herself. When she showed her friends the rag doll she made, they suggested she start selling them. She created an Etsy site and the dolls started selling like crazy.

Now in their second adoption, the Ducommuns are still using the dolls to help with the costs, selling them not only on Etsy but

The Ducommun Family - Craig, Laura & Zamara

One of the IkdKids Dolls

also through local shops in Flagstaff, Ariz.

Laura ships the custom ethnic dolls all over the world, and said she loves hearing the stories of each of her customers.

www.lkdKids.etsy.com

$ Amount Raised: Approximately $3,500

While waiting for their referral from Ethiopia, Debi Jenkins came up with the idea to make wooden Africa-shaped Christmas ornaments. Her dad is a woodworker and volunteered a lot of his time. He cut, Debi sanded and then she brought the ornaments home to paint and embellish. She's since started doing the woodwork herself. She sold several hundred ornaments to AmharicKids.com as well as to people all over the U.S. and Canada. Now she also makes magnets, keychains, wall hangings and more.

The Jenkins Family - Debi, Blake, Molly & Emily

www.etsy.com/shop/EthiopiaAdoption

$ Amount Raised: $2,000

- - - - - - - - - -

T-Shirts & Wearables

T-shirts seem to be the most popular item for adoptive families to sell, and there are some terrific designs. Some people have raised a few hundred dollars and others have raised thousands.

Most families find that having a few shirts printed up in various colors and styles and taking pre-orders is the way to go. This prevents you from having a bunch of unsold shirts lying around and wasting money. You'll pay more per shirt for your sample pieces, but it's worth the comfort knowing you won't have leftover stock.

Adoption-themed shirts seem to be a natural fit and are a common option. But don't limit yourself. Could you design, or have someone else design, a spirit shirt for your child's school and sell them to kids and parents? (You could even offer the school a portion of the proceeds for their PTF.) Or what about a shirt for your church?

If you're not artistically talented, don't worry. Most screen printing companies have designers working on staff that can take your idea and create a great design.

Bryce & Leanne Boddie of Texas raised approximately $2,500 with their adoption T-shirts. They gave shirts to all their immediate family and wore the shirts to church a lot to help spread the word. The Boddies also used the same design on reusable grocery bags, raising another $500 (approximately $5-10 profit per bag). They found that the bags also helped build an awareness about international adoption.

$ Amount Raised: T-shirts - $2,500; bags - $500

If you don't want to design your own shirt, there are a several other options.

Simply Love Fundraising Kit
Adoptive mom Kari Gibson created the first "Simply Love" T-shirt to help bring home their daughter, Zoie, from Ethiopia. She called her fundraiser a "total disaster" and it left her with boxes of unsold T-shirts. What she didn't know then, was that God would later use the Simply Love design to help dozens of adoptive families and people fundraising for missions.

© Simply Love

The Simply Love Fundraising kit includes 10 exclusive designs, with 23 different country options. The $49 kit gives you the designs, product ideas, and connects you with a special Simply Love screen printer who will give you wholesale prices. You can use the design on t-shirts, messenger bags, hats, water bottles and more. You choose your products, take pre-orders, purchase the items you need from the screen printing company, ship the items to the buyer and pocket the profit.

© Simply Love

www.mycrazyadoption.org

147 Million Orphans

147 Million Orphans' broad product line of T-shirts, jewelry, bags, and hats is available to adoptive families for fundraising. To apply, create an account on their website and ask your adoption agency to email them to confirm that you are a family actively pursuing adoption. Once completed, you will be approved to purchase products from www.147millionorphans.com at wholesale prices.

Their Adoption Fundraising Family Kit ($100) provides samples of several items so you can pre-sell the products. 147 Million Orphans suggests taking orders for products and then purchasing inventory in groups ($100 minimum per order) to avoid having leftover products. (Note: Not all items on their website are available for fundraising.)

Ugandan paper bead necklaces are their most popular item. The necklaces are made by women in Uganda who roll the beads from recycled paper, dip them in varnish and thread them onto string. (Prior to learning how to bead, most of the women picked trash or turned to prostitution to provide for their children.)

Adoptive families can sell 147 Million Orphan products for a 12-month period as long as they are still in process. Families have earned from $500-$10,000 for their adoptions.

www.147millionorphans.com

The Buoniconti family chose to just sell the paper bead necklaces from 147 Million Orphans and a few products from other organizations. Kryste took some of the necklaces and made earrings and bracelets out of them. They had a lot of repeat customers.

 Amount Raised: $500

Show Hope

Show Hope offers their shirts to adoptive families at wholesale prices. They provide pre-sale order forms to approved families. You pre-sell shirts for $25 and order them from Show Hope at the wholesale rate of $15. See the website for information on minimum quantities.
www.showhope.org/AdoptionAid/ShirtsOfHope.aspx

Adoption Bug

Adoptionbug.com gives a 25-45 percent commission (varies by design) to adoptive families who can choose up to six of their designs to sell. You can also submit up to two original art designs. Adoption Bug prints and ships the shirts for you. Adoptive families just submit the sign-up form, make their product selections, include a photo and a very brief bio. Adoption Bug creates a dedicated online store that you advertise to friends and family. There are no start-up or out-of-pocket costs.
www.adoptionbug.com

- - - - - - - - - -

Photography

As you share your adoption story, keep your ears open for offers of help from people who might have a skill you can use to raise funds. Photography is a perfect example!

If you know someone who is a photographer, ask if they would donate some of their time to raise funds for your adoption. There are several ways you could organize a photography event.

Portraits in the Park

Many photographers utilize a "portraits in the park" idea where they pick a picturesque location and book 20-30 minute sessions for family pictures, shooting eight or more different families in an afternoon. Set a suggested donation price for the portrait session and give each family a set number of high-resolution images on CD that they can take to any photo center for printing.

 Amount Raised: $250-$500

Studio-Style Portraits

If you have an indoor location that is suitable for setting up studio-style portrait sessions, schedule a family portrait day. Find a photographer to come and set up in your church or community center. Pre-sell portrait certificates for $20 that include the sitting fee and one free 8 x 10 portrait. The photographer will, of course, take multiple shots and allow the family to purchase additional photos. That's their incentive for offering their services to you and giving away the free 8 x 10. You keep the $20 session fee and they make money from selling additional portraits.

Russ and Katie Mohr are good friends with Jodie Allen
and Kim Weiss of with Fresh Art Photography in St. Louis.
When they heard about the Mohr's second adoption
they stepped forward to help them raise funds. Kim &
Jodie organized a day of mini-sessions for high-end kids
portraits. They had 20 slots offered at a discounted price
of $200, even sponsoring two slots and allowing people to
nominate deserving families. A friend in commercial real
estate development donated space in one of his venues.
The Mohrs supplied backdrops and food for the five
volunteers they had helping that day. Each family received
a disc of high-resolution images from their shoot.

 Amount Raised $5,000

The Mohr Family
Russ, Eliot, Katie & Dez (right)

Lori Stewart* used her own skills as a photographer to raise money for their adoption, organizing a family holiday portrait session at a local bookstore. She asked for a suggested donation of $20 for which the family received a free 5 x 7. Families could order a larger package and/or photo Christmas cards. Lori got the local photo lab to give her a discount on printing, which increased the Stewart's profit. The bookstore agreed to serve as the pickup location. The Stewarts advertised the event online, in the local newspapers and with flyers.

 Amount Raised: $2,000

Photography Magnets
Steve McKenzie's had a passion for photography for years and attempted to sell some of his photos as a fundraiser, but only had meager success. Then it occurred to him that maybe "smaller is better" and he began to make fine-art refrigerator magnets. At first they sold to their friends, then they launched 15000Refrigerators.com and began to network through social media. They sold over 5,000 magnets online and have magnets featured at four boutiques in Michigan.
http://www.15000refrigerators.com/

 Amount Raised: Ongoing

PictureMe Portrait Studio Fundraising Cards
If you want to save the work of coordinating photographers, locations and photo orders, you can use a more traditional route by selling fundraising cards for

Portrait Studios, which are located in most
ores nationwide.

You sell the cards for $10 each. When the customer
presents the card at the studio, they get a FREE 8 x 8
portrait and two enhanced 5 x 5 portraits with no sitting
fee. Your profit on each card depends on how many you
sell, but is a minimum of 50 percent.

This idea works best if you have a group of friends
who will help you sell the cards.

www.buyforcharity.com/walmart-photography-fundraiser-cards

$ Amount Raised: $5-$9 per card

- - - - - - - - - -

Recycle & Resell

Aluminum Recycling
The Morgan family
of Knoxville, Tenn.
has been collecting
aluminum cans and
foil for over a year.
Friends and family
(and THEIR friends
and family) have
joined the efforts,
including a few hair
salons that donate

The Morgan Family -
Jarred, Meredith, Mikayla & Jennifer

the foil they use to color hair. Twice the Morgans have had

"Can Our Yard" days where people dump their alumin_ __ collection on the Morgan's front lawn. Since Jarred is a youth minister, this is lots of fun for his students! The Morgans will also head over to the local college campus on game day and pick up cans. "The students may not realize at the time they are supporting us, but we'll take their cans anyway. We get a lot of strange looks, but we just chalk it up to being passionate about what God has called us to do!" said Jennifer. Whenever they have a truckload full they take it to the local recycling place.

 Amount Raised to Date: $1,800 (and still going)

Used Media Collection
Along with a garage sale and "Bags for ZaZa," the Crosby family had a used media drive. Linda emailed local friends and asked for any unwanted books, movies, video games, music CDs, curriculum and electronics.

Most of the items she sold on eBay. The items that didn't sell she took to a local media buyer; what they didn't buy was sold at the Crosby's garage sale.

 Amount Raised: $2,300

- - - - - - - - - - -

Luxury Linens
Sometimes a family's fundraising journey is so successful it turns into an ongoing business.

Through a unique set of events, the Lancaster family

received news that they could adopt the little girl from China they were sponsoring through an orphan care ministry. But with five kids and one income, they didn't know where to find the $26,000 they needed to bring Lori home.

A friend mentioned the idea of buying fine linens at wholesale and reselling them, and that was the start of Lori's Linens. Sales started off fairly slow until the Lancaster's circle of friends started to help them sell the sheets.

In 2010, the company sold over 570 sets of 1200-thread-count, Egyptian cotton sheets and helped the Lancasters bring Lori home. Now they help other adoptive families.

Lori's Linens provides order forms, a color chart and one sample set of sheets to use during sales. The cost to your family depends on how many orders you have, but ranges from $27-30 per set. Using Lori's Linens suggested retail price ($45), each set provides an average profit of $15-18. Families can increase the sales price if they want. *www.lorislinens.com*

Jacob and Susan Allee hit a fundraising wall, and were under a time crunch to raise funds to purchase their airline tickets to Ethiopia, when they heard about Lori's Linens. With the help of friends and other adoptive moms advertising on their blogs, the Allees quickly sold 80 sets of sheets.

 Amount Raised: $1,200 +

The Allee Family - Zoë, Susan, Jacob, Titus. Amo (top right) and Genet (bottom right) arrived home in late April 2011.

- - - - - - - - - -

Coffee

Your trips to Starbucks might be less frequent these days (if not, reread Chapter 5), but you can use those coffee cravings to raise money.

Just Love Coffee, founded by adoptive parents, sells fair trade coffee and puts a portion of their profits into projects in Ethiopia. Their adoption fundraising program gives you a customized order page where friends and family can order coffee. There is no up-front cost and all order fulfillment is handled by Just Love Coffee. You make $5 per bag and can continue selling for up to 12 months after your adoption is complete to help pay for post-placement costs. If you adopt a child with special needs who requires ongoing medical care, you can keep your store up indefinitely.

www.justlovecoffee.com

Jeremy & Rachel Fiet of Siloam Springs, Ark., made $150 in the first six months of their coffee fundraiser with JLC. The Fiets are adopting two children from Ethiopia.

Rachel & Jeremy Fiet

In addition to the Boddie family's online sales, they hosted a "coffee party." They ordered a couple of the sampler packs from Just Love Coffee so friends could try them before placing orders. (They also sold their adoption T-shirts and reusable grocery bags at the event.) They raised $500 that night and sold about $200 in coffee.

 Amount Raised: $150-$500+

- - - - - - - - - -

Direct Sales

Pampered Chef, Tupperware, Avon, Gold Canyon Candles, Premier Designs - dozens of companies employ independent sales consultants to sell their products through house parties and online catalog sales.

If you have a friend who is a consultant, ask if they would host a special party and donate the profits toward your adoption fund.

Better yet, gather several of these consultants right before the holidays for a special shopping event like Lara

Dinsmore did with her "Stop 'N Shop for Adoption" in early November. One of Lara's friends is a successful direct sales consultant; so it was her work and contacts that helped pull off the event. Each consultant that participated agreed to donate 50 percent of their commission to the Dinsmore's adoption fund. Lara's friend then followed up with each consultant after the event to collect the money.

Advertising for the Stop 'N Shop was done via Facebook, blogs and flyers.

 Amount Raised: $900

- - - - - - - - - -

Amazon.com Associates

Amazon offers an affiliate program that lets you earn money by promoting their products. Setting up an Amazon Associates account (www.affiliate-program. amazon.com) is quick and they provide you with easy instructions and widgets to use online.

Use your blog or website and link to specific products - books you're reading, top sellers, etc. Then spread the word to family and friends. You can also send them a link they can use ANY time they shop on Amazon.com that gives your Associate credit. Depending on the item and how many referral sales you make, you earn four to eight percent.

10
Puzzles, Prizes & Prints

Online Fundraising

Google "adoption blog" and you get over 24 million
results - blogs chronicling adoptions from the foster care
system, domestic private adoptions and adoptions of kids
from all over the world.

Having a blog is not only a great way to chronicle your
journey and preserve it for your family history, but it is a
great tool to raise awareness and funds.

Set up a PayPal account so that you can receive
donations toward your adoption. PayPal makes it super
easy to set up an account and use their merchant services
to add a "Donate Now" button right to your blog or
website. Make sure that your friends and family are aware
that donations to your fund via this method are not tax
deductible.

If later in your process you partner with a grant
organization that accepts donations on your behalf, you
will still want this option for T-shirt sales, giveaways or
auctions.

Many families break up their adoption costs into smaller sections and show a fundraising thermometer to track their progress. For example, you might say, "We need $2,000 to complete our application and home study." Once that goal is met, celebrate and then post the next goal, resetting your fundraising thermometer.

There are several places to get a fundraising thermometer for your blog; here's one to get you started: *www.easy-fundraising-ideas.com/tools/fundraising-thermometer/*.

Chip-In is an all-in-one "widget" that ties to your PayPal account and shows your goal and the amount raised (www.chipin.com).

Once you have the donation button set up, blog about your fundraising efforts. A lot of people are unaware of the cost of adoption and are curious about how the money is used. Be up front and honest with them and share from your heart.

- - - - - - - - - -

As people give general donations to your adoption fund, there are several ways to recognize them so that their investment in your journey is recorded for your future child. What a powerful testimony to how much he or she was loved even before they came to your family.

Puzzle Pieces

Many families purchase a 250-500 piece puzzle and, as people make donations toward the fund, write the person's name on the back of a puzzle piece. You might choose to divide your total adoption costs by the number of pieces so that a fully put-together puzzle equals a fully funded adoption. Or you might choose to use the puzzle to meet a smaller goal.

Periodic updates on your blog can show how the puzzle is growing; the pieces with names are connected upside down. Let people know how many pieces are still available. When the puzzle is completed, you get to reveal the picture on the other side which has been kept a surprise. The puzzle is then matted between two pieces of glass, framed and hung in the adopted child's room.

The Oberhauser family used their blog and a Facebook page titled "Bringing Home Vanya" to complete their puzzle. The completed puzzle now hangs in his room.

The Oberhauser Family - Joni, Isaac, Mark & Jimmy

Leaves of Love

Angela Elder was inspired by the puzzle piece idea, but wanted to create something unique that their future child would enjoy throughout their life. A friend mentioned the idea of using a fingerprint tree at her wedding and the Leaves of Love idea quickly sprouted in Angela's head.

She worked with the designers at Love
from the Thumb to create the "Leaves of
Love" fundraising tree.

   Adoptive families can choose from
three different trees and two different sizes
(11 x 17 or 24 x 36). Included in the kit is an
ink pack with four inks (3 shades of green
and one red) and a fine tip black marker.

   The tree can be used
in a variety of ways. You
can use it with online
donations, making a
fingerprint on the tree with
the donor's name for each
donation received. (Snap
a picture of their leaf and

email it with a thank you note.) You can also use your
tree during other fundraising events like garage sales and
benefit dinners, allowing more and more people to be part
of growing your family.
www.leavesoflove.blogspot.com

Quilt Pieces

The Halstead Family of New Prague, Minn., gave people
the opportunity to buy a fabric quilt square for $1 and then
sign their name or encouraging message on the square.
The squares, cut from donated fabric, were sold during a
couple of fundraising events and helped them raise $2,500.

   In the end, Jenna made one small quilt that they kept

for themselves, and used the rest of the squares to make quilts for the other children awaiting adoption at their child's orphanage. You could easily sell squares online as well and let people designate a message for their piece.

The Halstead Family - Carter, Phil, Mason, Charlotte, Jenna & Logan

 Amount raised: $2,500

Canvas Squares

Five weeks before their court date, the David family still needed $10,000 to pay all their adoption expenses. The bought a blank 24" x 30" canvas and divided it into 520 squares. Each square represented one $20 donation and the donor chose the color

The David Family
Becca, David, Huxley & Sakari

and/or message for the square. Using mostly social media to spread the word, the Davids exceeded their goal.

 Amount Raised: $11,075

- - - - - - - - - -

Giveaways

Blog giveaways are a fun way to raise money and can be as simple or complex as you want.

If you want something less time consuming, choose one or two popular items that you think would appeal to people - electronics for example.

With a little more time, you can gather a collection of items to give away and either choose to give the whole package to one winner, or draw names for each item.

Or you might have a series of giveaway contests for one item at a time. It's completely up to you.

Instead of paying for the item yourself, see if you can get a business or individual to donate the item. Some families use airline or other "point programs" to acquire giveaway items so that all the money raised goes directly toward the adoption. If you have friends who are photographers, hair stylists, massage therapists or other service industry people, ask if they would donate a gift certificate to the cause. Ask around and see if any friends have season tickets to the local professional sports team and would be willing to donate their seats to a game. The possibilities are endless.

Lara Dinsmore of Yuma, Ariz., collected over 35 items

The Dinsmore Family - Jon, Laura, Ellie & Cade

that became one huge prize pack in her "Give Thanks Giveaway" done during the Thanksgiving holiday. By sponsoring a piece of "the pie" for $10 (via a PayPal button on their blog), anyone could be entered in the drawing. People who purchased one of their adoption T-shirts received three additional entries. Anyone who sponsored a piece of the pie or bought a T-shirt and blogged about the giveaway received one additional entry.

All of the items in the giveaway prize pack were donated by friends and other adoptive families. Lara found that a lot of adoptive families with their own fundraisers were more than willing to give one of their T-shirts or hats.

Amount Raised: $470

Kryste Buoiconti decided to raffle off an American Girl Doll, allowing the winner to choose the specific doll. At first, she wasn't sure how successful the idea would be, hoping to clear $100 after paying for the doll. A $10 donation to their adoption fund equaled one entry; a $25 donation equaled three entries. She asked friends and family to blog about it and share it on Facebook. In one week, they had over 3,000 hits to their blog, received 80 donations and were totally blown away by the success of the giveaway.

Amount Raised: $2,375

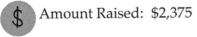

Online Auctions

You can take the traditional silent auction (see page 71) and easily make an online variation where people use blog comments to bid on individual items.

Jennifer and Trevor Chase of Southwest Missouri have two biological children and are adopting from Ethiopia. One of their most successful fundraisers was an online auction, birthed out of Jennifer's passion for crafty blogs.

Jennifer simply contacted craft bloggers she followed and friends who made handmade items, telling them about their adoption and the idea for an online auction. Some of the people she contacted also asked their own readers for additional items. In the end, Jennifer had over 80 items in her auction including clothing, jewelry, baby items and art work.

Some of the donors sent the items to Jennifer. Others just emailed a picture and then later mailed the item directly to the auction winner.

Jennifer set a one-week period for the auction and created a blog post for each auction item. The main blog entry contained a master list of all the auction items and a link to the respective blog post. Jennifer listed a starting price for each item equal to about 1/3 – 1/2 of the retail value. People entered their bid along with their name and email address in the comment section of the item in which they were interested.

Jennifer chose not to specify how much higher each bid needed to be but found that most people were generous. At the close of the auction, 70 of the items had sold and raised $1,200 for the Chase's adoption fund. Jennifer emailed each of the winners with payment instructions and then organized the shipment of all the items.

 Amount Raised: $1,200

The Elder family, who are adopting from Taiwan, had 60 items in their online auction - all donated by people that Angela contacted via websites and blogs.

Angela asked the donors to hold on to their items and agree to ship them directly to the auction winner. This not only saved the Elders a lot of time, but it saved them from having to pay the shipping expenses.

Their auction ran for a week. When there was 24 hours left, Angela added a new post with a list of items that hadn't been bid on to encourage her readers.

Angela says that keeping organized was the KEY! She had a spreadsheet keeping track of the donor's name, item, minimum asking price, final bid, winner's email address, shipping info and payment information.

 Amount Raised: $1,000

Christopher & Jennifer Wayman of Franklin, Tenn., had over 70 items in their online auction. Jennifer reached out to several of her favorite interior design bloggers to see if they would blog about the auction. While

Jennifer & Christopher Wayman

only two or three wrote blog posts, many of them agreed to advertise the auction via Facebook or Twitter. On one day, they had over 25,000 hits to the auction.

 Amount Raised: $2,600

11
Apply, Appeal & Accrue

Adoption Grants

There are over a dozen adoption grants available with varying requirements. Most require that your home study be complete, but you can apply for a few in the beginning stages of your adoption.

Most require the same basic financial information - income, debt and assets - so you'll save time if you gather all the information before you start. Because many of the applications are similar, you'll also save time if you fill them out in batches.

While it is time consuming and daunting, don't neglect this process because grants could provide quite a chunk of money for your adoption.

There are three basic types of grants - fundraising, direct and matching.

Fundraising grants give you an "account" with a non-profit grant organization to which people can donate. This provides your friends and family with the added benefit of a tax deduction when they give toward your adoption.

(Examples: Lifesong for Orphans, His Kids Too!)

Organizations that award you a flat amount toward your adoption expenses are direct grants. (Examples: Show Hope, Gift of Adoption, A Child Waits)

A matching grant combines fundraising and a direct grant. You receive a certain amount in matching funds if you raise an equal amount in donations from friends and family. A matching grant may encourage donations from others who give more readily because their gift doubles. (Examples: Lifesong for Orphans, Hand in Hand)

In all cases, the grant organization pays the money directly to "service providers," usually your adoption agency but some grants will pay money to travel agents.

These organizations award grants based on a lot of factors, including your family size, income and assets. Each organization has other requirements noted below.

This list is certainly not exhaustive, but contains the most well-known grants. You may also want to visit Resources4Adoption.com where Cherri Walrod does an amazing job of keeping up with the latest grants and has some great resources and e-books available.

Grant List

A Child Waits Foundation

Specifically designed to help older children and children with special needs, the A Child Waits (ACW) Grant Program helps families pursuing international adoption of these special children. The adoptive child must be over the age of five or have a medical or developmental need that makes the child harder to place. A home study and referral is required before filling out the pre-qualification form available on their website. Grant money is paid directly to the service providers (adoption agency, travel agent, etc.) and is disbursed just before the family is due to travel. The application process takes two to four months. Grant amounts vary but do not exceed $5,000. Application fee: None listed

www.achildwaits.org

Ava's Hope

Founded in 2005 by adoptive parents, Ava's Hope helps families who are adopting internationally. A volunteer-run organization, Ava's Hope allocates grant money as funds allow and only opens the application process at that time. Sign up for their e-news on their website to be notified of available grant money. Application fee: None listed

www.avashope.org

Both Hands Foundation

By partnering with Lifesong for Orphans, the Both Hands Foundation offers a unique grant opportunity. Approved adoptive families solicit fundraising sponsorship of a work day to benefit a widow in their community. For more information, see page 78.

www.bothhandsfoundation.org

Gift of Adoption

Gift of Adoption awards grants to families in the process of domestic and international adoptions. You must have

an approved and current home study from a licensed and accredited social worker. Those adopting internationally MUST be utilizing the services of a Hague-accredited adoption agency. Grants range from $1,000-$7,500 with the average award being $3,500. Application fee: $40
www.giftofadoption.org

God's Grace Adoption Ministry
Established in 1998, God's Grace Adoption Ministry (GGAM) uses matching grants to help adoptive families. Grants are available for Christian, two-parent families at any stage of the adoption process with a household income of $60,000 or less. Grant money is paid once a child (or children) is in the custody of the family and they submit outstanding adoption expenses that GGAM pays. The average grant amount is $2,500. Application fee: $10
www.ggam.org

Golden Dawn Adoption Assistance
Golden Dawn awards grants up to $2,000 to "Christian and LDS couples" adopting children with special needs. Application fee: $20
www.goldendawnaa.org

Hand in Hand
Hand in Hand helps families with matching grants. A completed home study and application is required. All grant money is disbursed directly to service providers. Application fee: None
www.handinhandadopt.org

Help Us Adopt
Private, domestic, international and foster care adoptions
are all eligible for grants from Help Us Adopt. Awarded
twice a year in June and December, grants range from
$500-$15,000, depending on individual family situations.
You must have a completed home study. Priority is given
to couples/individuals without children already in the
home. Grant money is paid directly to service providers
and must be used within one year. Application fee: None
www.helpusadopt.org

His Kids Too!
His Kids Too! allows your friends and family to make
tax-deductible donations toward your adoption expenses.
They are open ONLY to U.S. Citizens adopting children
from outside the U.S. No matching grants are available.
www.hiskidstoo.org

Katelyn's Fund
Katelyn's Fund provides grants to Christian couples
completing domestic or international adoptions.
Applicants must have a completed home study and be
interviewed by the board. Grants are typically $3,000 and
given as funds allow. Application fee: None
www.katelynsfund.org

Lifesong for Orphans
Lifesong enables friends and family to contribute to
your adoption and receive a tax deduction by offering
matching grants ranging from $1,000-$4,000. Their goal

is for children to be adopted into two-parent Christian families. Financial assistance is awarded based on need of the child, financial need of the parents, referral from and level of support from church leadership, leading of the Holy Spirit and availability of funds. If accepted, families receive a support fundraising kit to help them raise funds during a specific date range. (Lifesong also helps churches administer adoption funds for their members.)
www.lifesongfororphans.org

Little Flowers Foundation
Little Flowers Foundation (LFF) helps Catholic families with expenses related to adoption. Priority may be given to those with greatest financial need and those adopting children with special needs (developmental delays, older children, sibling groups, medical needs, etc.). LFF awarded $35,000 in grant money in 2010.
www.littleflowers.org

Lydia Fund
Available to Christian couples in the process of adopting internationally, applications for Lydia Fund grants must be made at least three months prior to travel. An interview is done before final approval. Selection for interviews is made within 90 days of application. Application fee: None
www.lydiafund.org

National Adoption Foundation

The National Adoption Foundation offers grants for all legal adoptions, and the only requirement is that a home study is in progress or completed. The board meets four times a year and awards grants ranging from $500-$2,500. Grant funds are disbursed directly to service providers. Application Fee: Donation of any amount
www.nafadopt.org

Orphan Impact

To be eligible for a grant from Orphan Impact, you must have been married for five years, have a yearly income from $30,000 - $80,000, be a high school graduate or have a GED, have a completed home study and complete the application process. NOTE: At press time, Orphan Impact was not accepting applications. Check their website for the latest information. Application Fee: None
www.orphanimpact.com

Our Creator's Hope

Based on availability of funds, Our Creator's Hope awards grants from $1,000 - $10,000. Married Christian couples with a completed home study are eligible to apply. Applications are reviewed on a quarterly basis, and grant money is paid to an approved 501(c)(3) adoption agency. Application Fee: None
www.ourcreatorshope.com

Parenthood for Me

Grants are available to U.S. Citizens pursuing adoption - either private or agency, either domestic or international. A completed home study is required. Families who already have children may apply. Grant money is dispensed to the service provider.

www.parenthoodforme.org

Sea of Faces

With grants ranging from $1,000-$3,000, Sea of Faces accepts applications from Christian couples with a completed home study and a referral for a child from a developing country. You must also have an approved I-171H or I-797C form. Two to three grants are awarded each quarter based on urgency of need, church involvement, overall financial stewardship and your adoption story. Families may apply up to six months after the child is home. Application Fee: $15

www.seaoffaces.org

Show Hope

Providing grants to Christian families and single parents, Show Hope has six application deadlines throughout the year. Applicants must have a completed home study and be in the process of adoption using a 501(c)(3) agency. Grants are awarded for both domestic and international adoptions. Application processing takes a minimum of 90 days, and priority is given to applicants with the greatest financial need. Application fee: None

www.showhope.org

The Micah Fund

The Micah Fund provides matching grants to Christian parents seeking to adopt minority children. Applicants must have a completed home study and be pre-qualified. If pre-qualified, a complete application is turned in and an interview conducted. Accepted families seek donations from friends and family to be matched by the Micah Fund. Grant money is disbursed to your placing agency after the placement of the child. Application Fee: None
www.micahfund.org

Some adoption agencies also have their own specific grants, so ask your caseworker.

Here is a list of a few grant organizations* that seek to help families in specific areas of the country or those in a specific targeted group.

- Adoption Funds for Ministers - Southern Baptist Ministers and Missionaries
  www.sbcadoption.com
- Caroline's Promise - North & South Carolina
  www.carolinespromise4u.org
- Ibsen Network - Washington State
  www.ibsenadoptionnetwork.com
- Kinsman Redeemer - Missouri
  www.thekinsmanredeemer.org
- Kyle Reagan Foundation - Indiana & Tennessee
  www.kylereagan.org

- Titus Task Foundation - Northwest Arkansas
  www.thetitustask.com
- Topeka Community Foundation - Kansas
  www.topekacommunityfoundation.org

*This grant list is informational and should not be construed as direct recommendations.

- - - - - - - - - - -

Fundraising Letters

If you receive a fundraising grant or a matching grant, you'll need to write a fundraising letter. Most grant organizations provide a sample letter and may give you some specific language to use for the giving instructions.

Admittedly, asking for money is never easy. Instead of thinking of it as asking for help, think of it as giving others an opportunity to serve an orphan. You are not raising money to add a child to your family; you are raising money to give a child a family. Often people want to help orphans but don't know how they can make a difference outside of adopting themselves.

Write your letter from your heart and reflect your family and your journey. Many families include a few frequently asked questions about adoption and why it costs so much.

In your letter, you should not only ask for donations to your adoption fund, but you should use this opportunity to ask if they could help you raise money in other ways. If they cannot give financially, can they help you with a garage sale or spaghetti-dinner fundraiser? Do they have a talent, like photography, that they could use to help you raise funds?

We received a fundraising grant for our adoption, and we used the opportunity to ask our friends and family to pray for us and for Wendemagegn, Beza and their grandmother.

Even if you don't have a fundraising grant, you can still send out letters. Just be sure people know their donation is a gift to directly to you and not eligible for a tax donation.

Kenny & Catherine Besk sent out about 100 letters and received over $15,000 in gifts toward their adoption. While they received three gifts of over $1,000, most donated from $20-$200. It all adds up.

12
Faith, Favor & Family

Besides applying for one fundraising grant, we applied for a couple of direct grants, but unfortunately, our previous year's income taxes made us look a lot better off financially than we were.

I admit I became discouraged when we were turned down, and I wondered how God planned on working this whole debt-free adoption thing out.

We originally thought we would have the kids home in July or August of 2008. Though we could not see the blessing in it at first, problems with our agency and paperwork made us miss this date and eventually get caught in the Ethiopian court closure. (Each year from August through October, the courts close due to the rainy season. If a judge has not heard your case before then, you just have to wait until they reopen.)

I remember crying when I heard that we would be delayed. I pictured all the summer clothes hung in closets upstairs that would most likely be too small by the next year. I was angry that a simple missed signature ruined

MY plans. (Did I mention I'm a bit of a control freak?)

I consoled myself with the knowledge that the kids would have more time with their grandmother. Plus, the extra months gave us more time to raise the money we needed to finish the adoption. (OK, maybe God DID know what He was doing.)

We had a few weekend "eBaypoloozas" where Mark and I photographed and listed items on eBay. Some were left over from the garage sale, some were from Mark's parents' house and some were from our own clutter. We added at least another $1,000 to the adoption fund.

Our court date was finally set for November 28th, the day after Thanksgiving.

Thanksgiving Day I was a bundle of nerves, but giddy at the same time. One moment I was completely confident we were going to pass court; the next I tried to temper my enthusiasm lest I be disappointed. In the prior weeks, a lot of families did not make it through court on their first try.

That night I took my cell phone upstairs and laid it on my nightstand with the ringer on as loud as it would go. I knew our agency caseworker, Grace, would call or text the moment she knew something. With the time difference between the States and Ethiopia, that could be the wee hours of the morning.

Mark woke up at the crazy hour of 4 a.m. to hit the Black Friday sales. As usual, I didn't hear a thing when he left. When I first stirred at 6:30, I glanced at my phone. There it was – a text message from Grace sent at 4:31 a.m.

"It was early today!! You have been approved!"

I'm sure I let out a squeal before I quickly dialed Mark and told him the good news. Then I tried to figure out whom else I could call at that crazy hour. Luckily, my best friend, Kristen, lives on the East Coast; so I called her next. Then I realized that Stacey was out hitting the early-bird sales too, so I called her and heard her sister and mom shout their excitement as they stood in line at Kohl's.

I lay in bed for awhile, thinking I could go back to sleep. Ha! So I finally got up and went downstairs, straight to the computer. All week I had worked on the announcement video for my blog - the first time I would be able to publicly share the kids' pictures. I typed up a quick message to go with it and hit the publish button. It was the most amazing feeling!

Passing court was an answer to prayer, but now the final agency fee was due and $8,000 in travel expenses were looming. With the income I made from freelance jobs and donations to our adoption fund, we were SOOOO close to our goal.

We just needed $3,000.

Several months prior, I volunteered to redesign the website for our adoption agency. Being a small agency, their website needed improvement and I offered my services as a volunteer. I had worked on it for several weeks when our case manager mentioned that the director said he would give us a discount on our agency fee for my work.

Awesome! Totally not expected, and certainly not my motivation, but I wasn't going to turn it down.

They never asked me how much I would normally

charge for the job. I thought about giving them a figure, but I felt God telling me not to worry about it. Whatever they offered would be a bonus, even if it was only a couple hundred dollars. Nothing more was said.

A few days after we passed court, our case manager called and said the director was applying a $3,000 credit to our agency fee for the website redesign.

And there it was.

Our complete adoption costs, miraculously provided for by God!

Epilogue

December 22, 2008

It's hard to describe how it feels to go a year missing part of your family. At restaurants, I would think about how we'd need a bigger table. During worship at church, I would imagine Wendemagegn and Beza standing next to me in the dimly-lit auditorium. At bedtime, I would imagine tucking in two more children.

Finally, we were in Ethiopia and the day arrived.

I'd slept surprisingly well, despite the music coming through our hotel room wall and the prayers over the loudspeaker in the early morning.

We dressed and tried to eat breakfast although my stomach seemed to just lurch around in my torso.

The drive to the orphanage was a strange mix of anticipation and fear. Would they run and give us a hug? Would they be scared? Would they recognize us from the pictures we sent? Would they cry? Would we cry?

As the gates opened and the driver pulled his car into

the courtyard, my eyes quickly scanned the faces in the crowd of kids, but I couldn't find them.

Turns out, they were at one final medical appointment required by the U.S. Embassy.

The next 90 minutes were the longest in my life. We finally watched the gate open and the kids walk in with one of the agency staff. They headed into another building, and I can only imagine the scene as the other kids besieged them to announce that their new parents were waiting.

A few moments later, they walked into the room where we waited. Shyly and quietly, they hugged us and sat as we made small talk. I don't even remember what I said. I'm sure it was all completely inane and inadequate.

For in that moment, our dream was realized.

We were together.

We were a family.

December 27, 2008 - The day we had been waiting for.

The Gumm Family - Noah, Beza, Julie, Mark, Natalie & Wendemagegn, who now goes by Luke.

Natalie, Noah, Luke & Beza have truly become siblings. They sometimes share, sometimes squabble, sometimes tease and sometimes annoy each other. I consider that a sure sign of "normalness" - whatever that is.

Beza, 10   Luke, 11

The Story Continues

Truly, I will never consider this book complete, as I continue to find fantastic fundraising ideas that adoptive families are using to bring their kids home.

That's why I've created a companion website at **www.adoptwithoutdebt.com** where I'll post new ideas, give tips on making your fundraising successful and let YOU share YOUR story.

You can also subscribe to the Facebook page at www.facebook.com/adoptwithoutdebt

I hope you'll stop by and join the conversation!

Julie

ADOPT WITHOUT DEBT WORKSHOP

The "Adopt Without Debt" Workshop is a 2.5 hour presentation that includes: how to find more money in your budget, adoption grants and creative fundraising ideas. A shorter one hour presentation title "Creative Fundraising Ideas" is also available. I'm available to adoption agencies, church ministries and non-profit organizations. For more information on fees and availability, please e-mail julie@adoptwithoutdebt.com.

What Others Are Saying

"We were thrilled to have Julie at our seminar in Birmingham. She has so much wisdom and insight to offer families considering the adoption process and those in the middle of it. We were overwhelmed by the attendance at our event and thrilled to hear from our families how Julie's presentation encouraged them and inspired them to use her methods in their own adoption stories. This seminar was so effective – we are ready to book her for another event next year!"
- Kate Anderson, Lifeline Children's Services

"Great presentation! So encouraging to hear so many fresh ideas and success stories. Very motivating." - Attendee

"Entertaining and enjoyable." – Attendee

"So much good and encouraging info!"- Attendee

Appendix

Books

"Total Money Makeover" by Dave Ramsey
"Family Feasts for $75 Per Week" by Mary Ostyn
"Supper's on the Table, Come Home" by Rachel Masters
      http://www.schallertel.net/~rmasters

Meal Planning & Coupons

E-Mealz - http://e-mealz.com
Coupons.com - http://print.coupons.com
Coupon Mom (free) - http://www.couponmom.com
Coupon Sense (fee-based) - http://couponsense.com
The Grocery Game (fee-based) - http://grocerygame.com

Other Sites Mentioned

Just Love Coffee - www.justlovecoffee.com
Simply Love - www.mycrazyadoption.org
147 Million Orphans - www.147millionorphans.com
Show Hope - www.showhope.org
Adoption Bug - www.adoptionbug.com
Leaves of Love - www.leavesoflove.blogspot.com
Resources4Adoption - www.Resources4Adoption.com

Sample Budget

This is Dave Ramsey's "Quickie Budget Form" - a great place to start. For instructions and more forms, go to *www.daveramsey.com/tools/budget-forms/*

The Basic Quickie Budget

Item	Monthly Total	Payoff Total	How Far Behind	Type of Account
GIVING	_____		_____	_____
SAVING	_____		_____	_____
HOUSING				
First Mortgage	_____	_____	_____	_____
Second Mortgage	_____	_____	_____	_____
Repairs/Mn. Fee	_____		_____	_____
UTILITIES				
Electricity	_____		_____	_____
Water	_____		_____	_____
Gas	_____		_____	_____
Phone	_____		_____	_____
Trash	_____		_____	_____
Cable	_____		_____	_____
*Food	_____		_____	_____
TRANSPORTATION				
Car Payment	_____	_____	_____	_____
Car Payment	_____	_____	_____	_____
*Gas & Oil	_____		_____	_____
*Repairs & Tires	_____		_____	_____
Car Insurance	_____		_____	_____
*CLOTHING	_____		_____	_____
PERSONAL				
Disability Ins.	_____		_____	_____
Health Insurance	_____		_____	_____
Life Insurance	_____		_____	_____
Child Care	_____		_____	_____
*Entertainment	_____		_____	_____
OTHER MISC.	_____		_____	_____

TOTAL MONTHLY NECESSITIES   _____

© Dave Ramsey

Employer Adoption Reimbursement

Many companies offer adoption reimbursement as part of their benefit package so ask your human resources department. For a list of "adoption-friendly" companies visit the Dave Thomas Foundation website under "Our Programs > Adoption Friendly Workplace."
www.davethomasfoundation.org/Home

If your workplace doesn't offer adoption benefits, talk to your supervisor or the personnel department about becoming an adoption-friendly workplace. The Dave Thomas Foundation offers a free toolkit to make it easy to propose and help your company establish an adoption benefits policy.
www.davethomasfoundation.org/Free-Adoption-Resources/ Adoption-Benefits

Military
Military service members who adopt a child under 18 years of age may be reimbursed qualified adoption expenses up to $2000 per adoptive child (up to a total of $5000 if more than one child is adopted) per calendar year.
www.militaryfamily.org/your-benefits/adoption/

Garage Sale Flyers

I created this poster in Mac Pages, saved it as PDF and emailed it to friends and family. We collected donations for two months and raised $5,200 at our garage sale.

I also designed a poster to advertise the event to our friends and family. However, the majority of our customers came from neighborhood signs.